AJIT DASH

in **36** HOURS

CHATGPT | GENERATIVE AI

The Step-by-Step Guide

For

OpenAI

&

Azure OpenAI

LEARN CHATGPT | PROMPT ENGINEERING | TEXT GENERATION | EMBEDDING | PLAYGROUND | CHAT | COMPLETIONS | MODEL FINE TUNING | MODEL TRAINING | FILTERING | INSTALLATION & MORE ...

WITH RECOMMENDATIONS |BEST PRACTICES | INDUSTRY USE CASES | QUIZ

FIRST EDITION

CHATGPT | GENERATIVE AI

The Step-By-Step Guide

For OpenAI & Azure OpenAI In 36 Hrs.

BY AJIT DASH

Dedicated to Almighty

Table of Contents

CHAPTER SUMMARY

Chapter 1: Introduction to OpenAI and Azure OpenAI - Exploring OpenAI's mission, Azure OpenAI's features, benefits, and differences between OpenAI and Azure OpenAI.

Chapter 2: Understanding AI and ML - Delving into artificial intelligence and machine learning, key components, and the role of deep learning and neural networks.

Chapter 3: Introduction to NLP - Basics of natural language processing, techniques like tokenization and text classification, and language model applications.

Chapter 4: Exploring GPT Models - Overview of GPT models, details of GPT-3 and GPT-4, their architecture, capabilities, and differences, including GPT-3.5 Turbo and Codex.

Chapter 5: How Tokens Work - Understanding tokens in GPT models, their benefits, and examples of successful Azure OpenAI implementations.

Chapter 6: Installation of OpenAI - Setting up an OpenAI account, exploring OpenAI product offerings, understanding ChatGPT, DALL-E 2, and APIs.

PREFACE

In the realm of technology and innovation, there are moments that redefine human progress. This book invites you to embark on a journey through one such epoch-shaping landscape: the world of OpenAI and Azure OpenAI services. As you turn these pages, you're delving into a realm where artificial intelligence converges with human ingenuity, where algorithms dance with creativity, and where the future takes shape in lines of code.

This comprehensive guide is designed to help you master OpenAI and Azure OpenAI services in just 36 hours! Whether you're a professional looking to expand your AI skills or a beginner eager to dive into the world of artificial intelligence, this book is your ultimate resource.

In this **Step-by-Step Guide**, you'll find clear and concise instructions, practical examples, and hands-on exercises that will accelerate your learning journey. From understanding the fundamentals of AI, OpenAI, Azure OpenAI & Machine learning to exploring natural language processing and building chatbots, you'll gain the knowledge and confidence to apply these technologies in real-world scenarios.

Carefully structured approach ensures that you can make the most of your time, with each chapter building upon the previous one to deepen your understanding and practical skills. By the end of the 36-hour journey, you'll have a solid foundation in OpenAI and Azure OpenAI, empowering you to leverage these cutting-edge technologies effectively.

Prepare to be inspired, challenged, and enlightened. Each concept demystified, each example dissected, and each exercise undertaken is a step closer to mastery. This book isn't just about learning; it's about embracing the future, one where AI amplifies human potential and propels us into new dimensions of innovation.

So, with curiosity as your compass and these pages as your guide, let's embark on a journey that will reshape how you view AI, expand the horizons of your expertise, and inspire you to contribute to a world where technology knows no bounds."

USING THIS BOOK AND BENEFITS GUIDELINES -WHOM IS THIS BOOK FOR

Welcome to your comprehensive guide to mastering OpenAI and Azure OpenAI services in just 36 hours! **This** book is your passport to the dynamic world of artificial intelligence, tailored for both beginners and professionals. Whether you're seeking to expand your AI skills or take your first step into the AI realm, this resource is designed to be your trusted companion.

Learning Path

The structured approach paves the way for an efficient learning journey. With each chapter building upon the previous one, you'll gradually delve deeper into AI concepts and applications. This journey is flexible, allowing experienced learners to dive into specific sections while ensuring beginners follow a well-guided path.

Hands-On Engagement

Embrace practicality through hands-on exercises and illustrative examples. These provide real-world experience, bridging theory and application seamlessly. Code snippets and interactive scenarios encourage you to engage directly with the content.

Real-World Relevance

The relevance of each chapter is rooted in real-world application. From understanding the basics of AI and Azure OpenAI to crafting AI-powered chatbots and exploring advanced AI applications, you'll gain the insights to innovate across industries.

Reflection and Reinforcement

End-of-chapter summaries consolidate key takeaways, anchoring your learning. Reflections encourage you to internalize what you've learned before moving forward, ensuring a solid foundation.

Benefits

This book unlocks a host of benefits:

1. Efficiency: Condensed into a focused 36-hour framework, you gain maximum knowledge in minimal time.

2. Practicality: Exercises and examples empower you with skills you can apply immediately.

3. Versatility: The content encompasses AI essentials and advanced applications, catering to diverse learners.

4. Confidence: With each chapter, your confidence grows to wield OpenAI and Azure OpenAI services effectively.

5. Continued Growth: Your acquired skills are future-proof, ready to adapt to AI's evolving landscape.

This book is your gateway to embracing AI's potential. Embark on this transformative journey with curiosity and an open mind, as we dive into the exhilarating world of OpenAI and Azure OpenAI services."

Chapter 1

Introduction to
OpenAI and Azure OpenAI

Section 1.1: Overview of OpenAI and Its Mission

OpenAI is a leading organization at the forefront of artificial intelligence research and development. Its mission is to ensure that artificial general intelligence (AGI) benefits all of humanity. OpenAI aims to build safe and beneficial AGI systems that can outperform humans in a wide range of economically valuable tasks while prioritizing ethical considerations.

OpenAI is known for its cutting-edge language models like GPT-3 (Generative Pre-trained Transformer 3) and GPT-4. OpenAI's primary goal is to ensure that artificial general intelligence (AGI) benefits all of humanity and is developed in a safe and ethical manner. OpenAI offers access to its models and technologies through APIs and partnerships.

Section 1.2: Introduction to Azure OpenAI and Its Features

Azure OpenAI is a powerful platform that brings the capabilities of OpenAI to developers and businesses. It provides a suite of services and tools that enable developers to leverage the power of artificial intelligence and natural language processing in their applications.

Azure OpenAI, on the other hand, is a specific offering within Microsoft Azure, Microsoft's cloud computing platform. Azure OpenAI provides access to OpenAI's models and services through the Azure platform. It allows developers and businesses to leverage OpenAI's powerful AI capabilities within the Azure ecosystem. Azure OpenAI provides a range of AI services, including natural language processing (NLP) capabilities, chatbot development tools, and content generation tools.

Azure OpenAI offers a user-friendly interface and integration with other Azure services, making it easy to incorporate AI capabilities into existing workflows.

Section 1.3: Benefits and Applications of OpenAI in Various Domains

The applications of OpenAI are vast and span across numerous domains. In the field of healthcare, OpenAI can assist in medical diagnosis, drug discovery, and personalized treatment recommendations. In finance, it can be used for fraud detection, risk analysis, and algorithmic trading. OpenAI also plays a significant role in customer support, content generation, chatbots, and virtual assistants.

OpenAI's language models, such as GPT-3 and GPT-4, have demonstrated remarkable capabilities in understanding and generating human-like text. They have been employed in content creation, writing assistance, language translation, and much more. These models have the potential to transform how we communicate, learn, and interact with technology.

By harnessing the power of OpenAI, businesses can automate repetitive tasks, gain valuable insights from large datasets, and provide personalized experiences to their customers. OpenAI's technologies have the potential to revolutionize industries, increase productivity, and drive innovation.

Throughout this book, we will explore the intricacies of OpenAI and Azure OpenAI, diving into the technical aspects and practical use cases. By the end, you will have a comprehensive understanding of how OpenAI and Azure OpenAI can be leveraged to create intelligent and impactful solutions in your domain.

So, let's embark on this journey together and unlock the potential of OpenAI and Azure OpenAI to shape the future of artificial intelligence and its applications!

Section 1.4: Major Differences Between OpenAI and Azure OpenAI:

1. Security & Data Privacy:

- **OpenAI:** OpenAI takes data security and privacy seriously. They have measures in place to protect user data and ensure compliance with applicable privacy regulations. However, as OpenAI is primarily focused on AI research and models, the responsibility for data security lies with the users and developers.

- **Azure OpenAI:** As part of Microsoft Azure, Azure OpenAI prioritizes security and data privacy. Azure has extensive security measures, including data encryption, access controls, and compliance certifications. Azure follows industry best practices to protect customer data and offers comprehensive tools for managing data privacy and security.

2. Compliance:

- **OpenAI:** OpenAI maintains compliance with relevant laws and regulations related to AI research and development. They emphasize responsible AI practices and ethical considerations but may not have the same level of compliance certifications as a cloud platform.

- **Azure OpenAI:** Azure OpenAI, being part of the Azure platform, adheres to a wide range of compliance standards, including GDPR, ISO 27001, HIPAA, and more. Azure provides compliance documentation, audit reports, and compliance tools to assist customers in meeting their compliance requirements.

3. Reliability:

- **OpenAI:** OpenAI strives to provide reliable AI models and research outcomes. However, the availability and reliability of their services may vary, as OpenAI's primary focus is on advancing AI technology and not on providing a production-ready cloud platform.

- **Azure OpenAI:** Azure is known for its high reliability and robust infrastructure. Azure OpenAI leverages Azure's infrastructure, which offers industry-leading uptime, scalability, and fault-tolerant services. Customers can rely on Azure's SLAs and global availability zones for their AI applications.

4. Responsible AI:

- **OpenAI:** OpenAI emphasizes responsible AI practices, fairness, and transparency in AI development. They actively work on addressing bias, ethical considerations, and potential risks associated with AI models. OpenAI promotes research and initiatives for ensuring AI benefits all of humanity.

- **Azure OpenAI:** Azure OpenAI inherits Microsoft's commitment to responsible AI. Microsoft has established principles and guidelines for ethical AI development, ensuring fairness, accountability, and transparency. Azure provides tools like Azure Machine Learning Interpretability to help developers understand and mitigate biases in AI models.

5. Holistic Solution:

- **OpenAI:** OpenAI focuses primarily on AI research, models, and AI development tools. While they offer advanced AI models like GPT, they may not provide a comprehensive platform for end-to-end AI solutions.

- **Azure OpenAI:** Azure OpenAI provides a holistic solution by integrating OpenAI models and services into the Azure cloud platform. It offers a wide range of AI services, tools, and resources that enable developers to build, deploy, and manage AI applications at scale. Azure provides a complete ecosystem for AI development, including data storage, processing, training, and deployment capabilities.

Section 1.4.1: Comparison Table:

Parameter	OpenAI	Azure OpenAI
Organization	Independent AI research organization	Part of Microsoft Azure platform
Mission	Development and promotion of AI technologies	Integration of OpenAI technologies into Azure
Research Focus	Advancing AI, AGI, and AI safety	AI models, services, and tools for Azure users
AI Models	Develops advanced AI models like GPT	Incorporates OpenAI models into Azure services
Accessibility	Accessible to researchers and developers	Accessible to Azure customers
Deployment	Provides AI research and models	Integration of OpenAI in Azure cloud environment
Services and Tools	Limited to OpenAI's offerings	Azure services tailored for AI tasks
Scalability	Dependent on OpenAI's infrastructure	Leverages Azure's scalable cloud platform
Support	OpenAI community and resources	Azure customer support and documentation
Pricing	OpenAI pricing model	Azure pricing model

Parameter	OpenAI	Azure OpenAI
Security & Data Privacy	Data security responsibility lies with users and developers[1]	Extensive security measures and compliance certifications. Enterprise Security, RBAC, Customer-Managed Keys[2]
Compliance	Compliant with relevant AI laws and regulations	Adheres to various compliance standards such as GDPR, ISO 27001, HIPAA, OC2, ISO, CSA STAR etc.[3]
Reliability	Availability and reliability may vary	High reliability and robust infrastructure with industry-leading up time. Azure SLA
Responsible AI	Emphasizes responsible AI practices and ethical considerations	Microsoft's principles and guidelines for ethical AI development. Built-in, Global compliance
Holistic Solution	Primarily focused on AI research LLM, image Generation and models	Comprehensive AI services, Complete PaSS solutions and tools

Best Practices:

1. Prioritize security and data privacy: Implement robust security measures and follow best practices to protect sensitive data when working with OpenAI or Azure OpenAI.

2. Ensure compliance: Understand the applicable regulations and standards for your industry and ensure that your AI applications adhere to them. Azure OpenAI

---

[1] https://openai.com/security

[2] https://learn.microsoft.com/en-us/legal/cognitive-services/openai/data-privacy

[3] https://learn.microsoft.com/en-us/azure/compliance/

provides comprehensive compliance documentation and tools to assist with this.

3. Consider reliability: Evaluate the reliability requirements of your AI applications. Azure OpenAI, with its robust infrastructure and service-level agreements, can provide the necessary reliability for mission-critical projects.

4. Practice responsible AI: Mitigate biases, ensure fairness, and promote transparency in AI development. Both OpenAI and Azure OpenAI emphasize responsible AI practices, but Azure provides additional resources and guidelines to support developers.

5. Leverage the holistic solution: Azure OpenAI offers a complete ecosystem for AI development, including data storage, processing, training, and deployment capabilities. Utilize these resources to streamline your AI workflow.

6. Stay updated with advancements: Keep abreast of the latest developments, resources, and best practices in the field of AI. OpenAI and Azure regularly release updates and provide documentation and guides to help developers leverage their offerings effectively.

SUMMARY & CONCLUSION (CHAPTER 1)

In summary, OpenAI is the research organization that develops advanced AI models, while Azure OpenAI is the platform that integrates OpenAI's models and services into the Microsoft Azure cloud computing environment. Azure OpenAI provides developers and businesses with convenient access to OpenAI's AI technologies, making it easier to build and deploy AI-powered applications and solutions.

In conclusion, both OpenAI and Azure OpenAI offer valuable resources and capabilities for AI development. OpenAI focuses on AI research and models, while Azure OpenAI provides a comprehensive cloud platform with additional features and services. By considering the specific needs of your project, you can make an informed decision on which option is best suited for your AI endeavors.

Note All the models in the OpenAI are available in Azure OpenAI and Azure Cloud infrastructure are enterprise grade compliance are available in the Azure OpenAI.

By following these best practices, you can maximize the benefits of OpenAI and Azure OpenAI, ensuring the security, compliance, reliability, responsible AI practices, and holistic development of your AI applications.

CHAPTER 1 QUIZ: TEST YOUR SKILLS

1. What is the primary focus of OpenAI?

   a) Cloud infrastructure

   b) AI research and models

   c) Data storage and processing

   d) Compliance and security

2. Which cloud platform offers Azure OpenAI services?

   a) Google Cloud Platform

   b) Amazon Web Services

   c) Microsoft Azure

   d) IBM Cloud

3. True or False: OpenAI and Azure OpenAI prioritize security and data privacy.

4. What is the key benefit of using Azure OpenAI for AI development?

   a) Extensive compliance certifications

   b) Advanced AI research models

   c) Seamless integration with Google Cloud

d) Cost-effective pricing options

5. What does NLP stand for in the context of OpenAI?

a) Natural Language Programming

b) Neural Language Processing

c) Natural Language Processing

d) Neural Linguistic Programming

6. Which OpenAI model is widely known for its text generation capabilities?

a) GPT-2

b) GPT-3

c) GAN

d) LSTM

7. How does Azure OpenAI ensure reliability for AI applications?

a) By providing extensive compliance documentation

b) Through integration with Azure's robust infrastructure

c) By offering competitive pricing options

d) With real-time data analytics capabilities

8. True or False: OpenAI and Azure OpenAI promote responsible AI practices, including fairness, transparency, and accountability.

9. What is one use case for OpenAI's GPT models?

    a) Stock market prediction

    b) Weather forecasting

    c) Content generation

    d) DNA sequencing

10. What is the primary advantage of using Azure OpenAI over OpenAI directly?

    a) Access to advanced AI research models

    b) Seamless integration with third-party cloud platforms

    c) Greater control over data privacy and security

    d) Cost-effective pricing options

Answer for the Quiz check the Q/A section

CHAPTER 1 QUIZ: ANSWERS

Certainly! Here are the answers to the quiz questions:

1. What is the primary focus of OpenAI?

   Answer: b) AI research and models

2. Which cloud platform offers Azure OpenAI services?

   Answer: c) Microsoft Azure

3. True or False: OpenAI and Azure OpenAI prioritize security and data privacy.

   Answer: True

4. What is the key benefit of using Azure OpenAI for AI development?

   Answer: a) Extensive compliance certifications

5. What does NLP stand for in the context of OpenAI?

   Answer: c) Natural Language Processing

6. Which OpenAI model is widely known for its text generation capabilities?

   Answer: b) GPT-3

7. How does Azure OpenAI ensure reliability for AI applications?

Answer: b) Through integration with Azure's robust infrastructure

8. True or False: OpenAI and Azure OpenAI promote responsible AI practices, including fairness, transparency, and accountability.

Answer: True

9. What is one use case for OpenAI's GPT models?

Answer: c) Content generation

10. What is the primary advantage of using Azure OpenAI over OpenAI directly?

Answer: c) Greater control over data privacy and security

Chapter 2

Understanding Artificial Intelligence and Machine Learning

Section 2.1: Introduction to Artificial Intelligence

Artificial Intelligence (AI) is a field of computer science that focuses on creating intelligent systems capable of performing tasks that typically require human intelligence. These tasks include problem-solving, decision-making, perception, and language understanding. AI aims to develop machines that can mimic human cognitive abilities and exhibit intelligent behavior.

Section 2.2: Introduction to Machine Learning

Machine Learning (ML) is a subfield of AI that focuses on enabling machines to learn from data and improve their performance over time without being explicitly programmed. ML algorithms allow systems to automatically analyze and interpret complex patterns in data and make predictions or take actions based on that information.

Section 2.3: Key Components of Machine Learning

In machine learning, three key components work together to enable learning and prediction:

1. Models: Models represent the learned knowledge or understanding of the system. They capture the relationships between input data and the desired output or prediction. Models can take various forms, such as decision trees, support vector machines, or neural networks.

2. Data: Data is the fuel for machine learning algorithms. It consists of input examples or instances that the machine learning system uses to learn and make predictions. High-quality, diverse, and representative data is essential for training accurate and reliable models.

3. Algorithms: Algorithms are the mathematical and computational techniques that enable learning from data. They define how the model learns from the data and updates its internal parameters or structure to improve its performance. There are various types of machines learning algorithms, including supervised learning, unsupervised learning, and reinforcement learning.

Section 2.4: Overview of Deep Learning and Neural Networks

Deep Learning is a subset of machine learning that focuses on training deep neural networks, which are inspired by the structure and function of the human brain. Neural networks consist of interconnected layers of artificial neurons called nodes or units. Each node takes input, applies an activation function, and produces an output.

Deep neural networks have multiple hidden layers, allowing them to learn hierarchical representations of complex patterns in data. They excel in tasks such as image recognition, natural language processing, and speech recognition. Deep learning has achieved remarkable breakthroughs in various domains, thanks to its ability to automatically learn intricate features and representations from raw data.

Neural networks can be trained using large datasets, optimizing their parameters through a process called backpropagation. This process involves calculating the error between the predicted output and the desired output and adjusting the network's weights accordingly to minimize the error.

Throughout this book, we will delve deeper into the concepts of artificial intelligence and machine learning, exploring various algorithms, models, and techniques. We will also discuss real-world applications, challenges, and ethical considerations associated with these technologies. By the end, you will have a solid understanding of AI and ML and how they are transforming industries and shaping the future.

So, let's embark on this enlightening journey into the realm of artificial intelligence and machine learning, where the possibilities are vast, and the potential for innovation is limitless!

Best Practices:

Best Practices in Artificial Intelligence and Machine Learning:

1. Define clear goals: Clearly define the problem you want to solve or the objective you want to achieve using AI and ML techniques. Having well-defined goals helps guide the entire process.

2. Gather high-quality data: Data quality is crucial for training accurate and reliable models. Collect diverse, representative, and relevant data to ensure the model can generalize well to new examples.

3. Preprocess and clean the data: Data preprocessing involves handling missing values, removing outliers, and normalizing the data. Cleaning the data ensures that it is in the right format and free from errors or inconsistencies.

4. Choose appropriate algorithms and models: Select algorithms and models that are suitable for the problem at hand. Consider factors such as the type of data, the desired outcome, and the available computing resources.

5. Split data for training and evaluation: Divide your data into training and evaluation sets. Use the training set to train the model and the evaluation set to assess its performance. This helps in detecting overfitting and generalization issues.

6. Regularly evaluate and iterate: Continuously monitor and evaluate the performance of your models. Assess metrics such as accuracy, precision, recall, and F1 score. Iterate and refine your models based on the evaluation results.

7. Interpret and explain the model's decisions: In complex or sensitive applications, it is important to understand how the model arrives at its decisions. Use techniques such as feature importance analysis or model interpretability methods to gain insights into the model's inner workings.

8. Address bias and fairness: Be aware of potential biases in your data and models. Take steps to mitigate bias and ensure fairness in decision-making processes. Regularly audit and monitor for bias during model development and deployment.

9. Maintain proper documentation: Document the entire AI and ML development process, including data preprocessing, model selection, hyperparameter tuning, and evaluation results. Proper documentation helps in reproducibility, collaboration, and future reference.

10. Stay up to date with advancements: AI and ML are rapidly evolving fields. Stay updated with the latest research, techniques, and best practices. Attend conferences, read journals, and engage in professional networks to keep learning and growing.

By following these best practices, you can enhance the effectiveness and reliability of your AI and ML projects while ensuring ethical considerations and responsible deployment.

SUMMARY & CONCLUSION (CHAPTER 2)

In summary we introduce the concepts of artificial intelligence (AI) and machine learning (ML). AI focuses on creating intelligent systems that can perform tasks requiring human intelligence, while ML enables machines to learn from data and improve their performance without explicit programming. We discuss the key components of ML: models, data, and algorithms. Additionally, we explore deep learning and neural networks, which excel in tasks like image recognition and natural language processing. This chapter sets the foundation for further exploration of AI and ML in subsequent chapters, covering applications, challenges, and ethical considerations.

In conclusion, Chapter 2 provides an overview of artificial intelligence (AI) and machine learning (ML). We learn that AI focuses on creating intelligent systems capable of human-like tasks, while ML enables machines to learn from data and improve their performance. The key components of ML are models, data, and algorithms, which work together to enable learning and prediction. We also explore deep learning and neural networks, which are powerful techniques in ML. This chapter sets the stage for further exploration of AI and ML concepts, applications, challenges, and ethical considerations in the rest of the book.

CHAPTER 2 QUIZ: TEST YOUR SKILLS

Here's a quiz with 10 questions related to artificial intelligence and machine learning:

1. What is the primary goal of artificial intelligence?

    a) Replicate human intelligence

    b) Automate tasks

    c) Create intelligent machines

    d) Improve decision-making

2. Which component of machine learning represents the learned knowledge or understanding of the system?

    a) Data

    b) Algorithms

    c) Models

    d) Neural networks

3. What is the process of enabling machines to learn from data and improve their performance over time called?

a) Artificial intelligence

b) Data mining

c) Machine learning

d) Deep learning

4. Which type of machine learning algorithm uses labeled data to make predictions or classifications?

a) Supervised learning

b) Unsupervised learning

c) Reinforcement learning

d) Deep learning

5. What are neural networks inspired by?

a) Human brains

b) Animal behavior

c) Mathematical equations

d) Computer algorithms

6. What is the process of adjusting the weights of a neural network to minimize the prediction error called?

a) Back propagation

b) Forward propagation

c) Gradient descent

d) Weight optimization

7. What is the purpose of data preprocessing in machine learning?

    a) Cleaning and transforming data

    b) Selecting the most relevant features

    c) Handling missing values

    d) All of the above

8. What is the term for the division of data into training and evaluation sets during machine learning?

    a) Data splitting

    b) Data separation

    c) Data partitioning

    d) Data segregation

9. What does bias refer to in the context of machine learning?

    a) Unfairness in decision-making

    b) A type of algorithm

    c) Lack of accuracy

    d) Data inconsistency

10. Why is documentation important in AI and ML projects?

    a) For reproducibility and collaboration

    b) To meet regulatory requirements

c) For future reference and troubleshooting

d) All of the above

27

CHAPTER 2 QUIZ: ANSWERS

1. What is the primary goal of artificial intelligence?

   - Answer: a) Replicate human intelligence

2. Which component of machine learning represents the learned knowledge or understanding of the system?

   - Answer: c) Models

3. What is the process of enabling machines to learn from data and improve their performance over time called?

   - Answer: c) Machine learning

4. Which type of machine learning algorithm uses labeled data to make predictions or classifications?

   - Answer: a) Supervised learning

5. What are neural networks inspired by?

   - Answer: a) Human brains

6. What is the process of adjusting the weights of a neural network to minimize the prediction error called?

   - Answer: a) Backpropagation

7. What is the purpose of data preprocessing in machine learning?

- Answer: d) All of the above (cleaning and transforming data, selecting the most relevant features, handling missing values)

8. What is the term for the division of data into training and evaluation sets during machine learning?

- Answer: c) Data partitioning

9. What does bias refer to in the context of machine learning?

- Answer: a) Unfairness in decision-making

10. Why is documentation important in AI and ML projects?

- Answer: d) All of the above (for reproducibility and collaboration, to meet regulatory requirements, for future reference and troubleshooting)

Chapter 3

Introduction to
Natural Language Processing (NLP)

Section 3.1: Basics of Natural Language Processing and Its Importance

Natural Language Processing (NLP) is a branch of artificial intelligence that focuses on the interaction between computers and human language. It involves the analysis, understanding, and generation of human language, enabling machines to comprehend and process textual data in a way that is similar to how humans do.

NLP plays a crucial role in bridging the gap between human language and computer systems. It enables computers to understand, interpret, and derive meaning from unstructured textual data, such as emails, social media posts, articles, and customer reviews. By leveraging NLP techniques, businesses and organizations can unlock valuable insights, automate tasks, improve customer experiences, and make informed decisions.

Section 3.2: Key Techniques in NLP

3.2.1 Tokenization

Tokenization is the process of breaking down textual data into smaller meaningful units called tokens. Tokens can be individual words, phrases, sentences, or even characters. By tokenizing text, NLP algorithms can analyze and manipulate language at a more granular level. For example:

Original Text: "I love natural language processing!"

Tokenized Text: ["I", "love", "natural", "language", "processing", "!"]

3.2.2 Text Classification

Text classification is the task of assigning predefined categories or labels to textual data. It involves training a model on labeled examples to learn the patterns and characteristics associated with each category. For instance, classifying customer reviews as positive or negative sentiment:

Example:

Text: "The movie was amazing! I loved every minute of it."

Category: Positive Sentiment

Text: "The service was terrible. I had a horrible experience."

Category: Negative Sentiment

3.2.3 Sentiment Analysis

Sentiment analysis, also known as opinion mining, aims to determine the sentiment or emotional tone expressed in textual data. It can identify whether a piece of text expresses a positive, negative, or neutral sentiment. Sentiment analysis has numerous applications, such as social media monitoring, brand reputation management, and customer feedback analysis.

Example:

Text: "I'm extremely excited about the new product launch!"

Sentiment: Positive

Text: "I'm disappointed with the customer support. They were unhelpful."

Sentiment: Negative

Section 3.3: Overview of Language Models and Their Applications

Language models are a fundamental component of NLP. They are statistical models that learn the probabilities and patterns of language to generate coherent and contextually relevant text. Language models are extensively used in various NLP tasks, including machine translation, question answering, chatbots, and text generation.

One notable example of a language model is OpenAI's GPT (Generative Pre-trained Transformer) series, such as GPT-3. These models have achieved remarkable advancements in natural language understanding and generation. They are trained on vast amounts of text data and can generate human-like responses, write code, compose stories, and provide detailed answers to complex questions.

Language models have the potential to revolutionize how we interact with computers and consume information. They are empowering businesses to automate customer support, create personalized content, enhance language translation, and enable more natural conversational interfaces.

Throughout this book, we will dive deeper into the intricacies of natural language processing. We will explore advanced NLP techniques, delve into the workings of language models, and showcase real-world applications across various industries. By the end, you will have a comprehensive understanding of NLP and how it is transforming the way we communicate and interact with technology.

So, let's embark on this enlightening journey into the realm of Natural Language Processing, where the power of language meets the potential of AI, opening doors to endless possibilities and innovation.

Best Practices:

1. Define clear objectives: Clearly define the goals and objectives of your NLP project. Understand the problem you are trying to solve and the specific tasks you want to accomplish with NLP techniques.

2. Choose appropriate data: Select high-quality and representative data that is relevant to your NLP task. Ensure that the data is diverse and covers a wide range of scenarios to improve the accuracy and generalizability of your models.

3. Preprocess and clean data: Perform data preprocessing steps such as removing noise, handling missing values, normalizing text, and eliminating irrelevant information. Cleaning the data helps improve the quality of input for NLP models.

4. Use appropriate tokenization techniques: Tokenize text into meaningful units, such as words or sub words, to facilitate analysis and modeling. Consider using advanced tokenization techniques like Byte-Pair Encoding (BPE) or Word Piece for handling out-of-vocabulary words.

5. Implement effective feature engineering: Extract relevant features from the text that capture important information for your NLP task. This may include n-gram representations, TF-IDF, word embeddings, or contextualized word representations like BERT or ELMO.

6. Select suitable algorithms and models: Choose the appropriate algorithms and models based on your specific NLP task. Consider using traditional machine learning algorithms like Naive Bayes or SVM for simpler tasks, and deep learning models like recurrent neural networks (RNNs) or transformers for more complex tasks.

7. Train and fine-tune models: Train your NLP models on labeled data, and fine-tune them using techniques like cross-validation or hyperparameter optimization. Regularly evaluate the performance of your models on validation sets to identify areas for improvement.

8. Handle class imbalance and bias: Pay attention to class imbalance in your data and employ techniques like oversampling, under sampling, or class weighting to address the issue. Additionally, be aware of bias in your data and models and take steps to mitigate it to ensure fairness.

9. Regularly evaluate and monitor models: Continuously evaluate the performance of your NLP models on test data to assess their effectiveness. Monitor model behavior and performance in production to identify any drift or degradation and take corrective actions.

10. Stay up-to-date with advancements: Keep up with the latest research and advancements in NLP. Stay informed about new algorithms, models, and techniques that can enhance the performance and capabilities of your NLP applications.

By following these best practices, you can improve the effectiveness and reliability of your NLP projects and achieve better outcomes in understanding, analyzing, and generating human language.

SUMMARY & CONCLUSION (CHAPTER 3)

In summary Chapter 3 introduces Natural Language Processing (NLP) and its significance in enabling computers to understand and process human language. It covers key techniques such as tokenization, text classification, and sentiment analysis. The chapter also highlights the role of language models like OpenAI's GPT series. Overall, the chapter sets the stage for deeper exploration of advanced NLP techniques and real-world applications.

In conclusion, Chapter 3 provides an introduction to Natural Language Processing (NLP), its importance in enabling computers to understand and process human language, and its applications in various fields. The chapter covers key techniques in NLP, including tokenization, text classification, and sentiment analysis. It also highlights the significance of language models like OpenAI's GPT series in advancing NLP capabilities. Throughout the book, readers will gain a deeper understanding of advanced NLP techniques and explore real-world applications. By the end, they will have a comprehensive grasp of NLP's transformative potential in communication and technology.

CHAPTER 3 QUIZ: TEST YOUR SKILLS

1. What is Natural Language Processing (NLP)?

    a) A programming language

    b) A branch of artificial intelligence

    c) A data visualization technique

    d) A hardware component

2. What is the process of breaking down textual data into smaller meaningful units called?

    a) Segmentation

    b) Classification

    c) Tokenization

    d) Normalization

3. Which NLP task involves assigning predefined categories or labels to textual data?

    a) Sentiment analysis

    b) Text classification

    c) Named entity recognition

    d) Machine translation

4. What is the name of the language model developed by OpenAI that has achieved significant advancements in NLP?

   a) LSTM

   b) GPT-3

   c) CNN

   d) RNN

5. Which NLP technique aims to determine the sentiment expressed in textual data?

   a) Sentiment analysis

   b) Text summarization

   c) Topic modeling

   d) Named entity recognition

6. What is the process of adjusting a language model's internal parameters to minimize the error between predicted and desired outputs?

   a) Tokenization

   b) Normalization

   c) Backpropagation

   d) Dimensionality reduction

7. Which component of NLP is responsible for capturing the learned knowledge or understanding of the system?

   a) Algorithms

b) Data

c) Models

d) Features

8. Which type of machine learning algorithm is commonly used in NLP for supervised learning tasks?

a) Decision tree

b) Support vector machine

c) Random forest

d) K-means clustering

9. Which NLP technique focuses on automatically generating human-like text?

a) Sentiment analysis

b) Text classification

c) Text generation

d) Named entity recognition

10. What is the primary goal of NLP in bridging the gap between human language and computer systems?

a) Understanding human emotions

b) Analyzing complex linguistic structures

c) Enabling machines to comprehend and process textual data

d) Creating new languages for communication

CHAPTER 3 QUIZ: ANSWERS

1. What is Natural Language Processing (NLP)?

   Answer: b) A branch of artificial intelligence

2. What is the process of breaking down textual data into smaller meaningful units called?

   Answer: c) Tokenization

3. Which NLP task involves assigning predefined categories or labels to textual data?

   Answer: b) Text classification

4. What is the name of the language model developed by OpenAI that has achieved significant advancements in NLP?

   Answer: b) GPT-3

5. Which NLP technique aims to determine the sentiment expressed in textual data?

   Answer: a) Sentiment analysis

6. What is the process of adjusting a language model's internal parameters to minimize the error between predicted and desired outputs?

   Answer: c) Backpropagation

7. Which component of NLP is responsible for capturing the learned knowledge or understanding of the system?

Answer: c) Models

8. Which type of machine learning algorithm is commonly used in NLP for supervised learning tasks?

Answer: b) Support vector machine

9. Which NLP technique focuses on automatically generating human-like text?

Answer: c) Text generation

10. What is the primary goal of NLP in bridging the gap between human language and computer systems?

Answer: c) Enabling machines to comprehend and process textual data

Chapter 4

Exploring OpenAI GPT Models

Section 4.1: History and background of GPT models

The GPT models' evolution represents advancements in model size, training data, and performance, enabling more impressive language generation and understanding capabilities. The research and development of GPT models by OpenAI have significantly contributed to the field of natural language processing and AI-driven language models.

Model	Launch Date	Training Data	Number of Parameters	Max Sequence Length
GPT-1[4]	2018	Web pages and books	117 million	1024
GPT-2[5]	2019	Web pages and books	1.5 billion	2048

---

[4] https://cdn.openai.com/better-language-models/language_models_are_unsupervised_multitask_learners.pdf
[5] https://cdn.openai.com/better-language-models/language_models_are_unsupervised_multitask_learners.pdf

GPT-3[6]	2020-2021	Web pages and books, Common Crawl dataset, Wikipedia entries, and more.	175 billion	2048
GPT-4 (expected)	TBA	TBA	Estimated to be in trillions	TBA

Section 4.2: Introduction to OpenAI's GPT Models: GPT-3 and GPT-4

OpenAI's GPT (Generative Pre-trained Transformer) models have revolutionized the field of natural language processing. They are state-of-the-art language models that leverage deep learning techniques to understand, generate, and manipulate human language with astonishing accuracy and creativity.

The two prominent GPT models introduced by OpenAI are GPT-3 and GPT-4. These models have made significant advancements in language understanding, natural language generation, and context comprehension. They have been trained on vast amounts of diverse textual data, enabling them to grasp the nuances and intricacies of human language.

---

[6] https://cdn.openai.com/better-language-models/language_models_are_unsupervised_multitask_learners.pdf

Section 4.2: Understanding the Architecture and Capabilities of GPT Models

GPT models are built upon a transformer architecture, which allows them to capture long-range dependencies and contextual relationships in text. The transformer architecture consists of multiple layers of self-attention mechanisms, enabling the model to weigh the importance of different words and phrases within a given context.

These models can perform a wide range of language-related tasks, including text completion, summarization, translation, sentiment analysis, and question answering. They can generate coherent and contextually relevant text by predicting the next word or phrase based on the preceding context. GPT models have the ability to understand and generate human-like responses, write code snippets, create stories, and engage in meaningful conversations.

Section 4.3: What are the different GPT models available in Azure OpenAI?

GPT models have standard naming convention

```
{family} - {capability} [-{input-type}] - {identifier}
```

In summary, for a GPT model:

- Family: Refers to a group of models sharing similar architecture and characteristics.

- Capability: Relates to the model's ability to generate coherent and contextually relevant text.

- Input-type: Represents the type of data accepted by the model, typically textual information.

- Identifier: Unique label or name assigned to a specific version or variant of the model.

text – davinci – 003

Example:

{family} – {capability}[{identifier}

Model Capability	Token #	Used For	Power & Cost
Davinci	4096	Complex intent, cause and effect, summarization for audience, Content creation, translation	Expensive as compared to all other model. Slower processing than other models
Curie	2048	language generation, chatbots, question answering systems, text completion	Less expensive than Davinci but expensive than Babbage and Ada. Less powerful than Davinci
Babbage	2048	Semantic search & classification	Higher cost than Ada but less cost than Curie and Davinci. Also, less powerful than Curie and Davinci
Ada	2048	text parsing, address correction, and simple classification tasks.	Cheapest among all the model's family and less powerful
Davinci Codex	4096	Convert natural language to code	Powerful than Cushman and high cost
Cushman Codex		Convert natural language to code	Less powerful than Davinci and less cost

> This model is a GPT-3 text model, the most powerful (davinci), and of the latest version 003 version version (003)

Note:

Some of the model been deprecated: Deprecation of the model can be found in the following links

https://platform.openai.com/docs/deprecations

Foe Azure OpenAI GPT3 and GPT 3.5 models are not available for new deployment starting July 6th 2023

Section 4.4: GPT-3 Model Details7:

GPT-3, short for "Generative Pre-trained Transformer 3," is a state-of-the-art language model developed by OpenAI. It is the third iteration in the GPT series and represents a significant advancement in natural language processing and generation.

GPT-3 is based on a deep learning architecture known as a Transformer. It has been trained on a massive amount of diverse text data, including web pages, books, articles, and

---

[7] Deprecation of the model can be found in the following links
https://platform.openai.com/docs/deprecations
For Azure OpenAI GPT3 and GPT 3.5 models are not available for new deployment starting July 6th 2023

more. With 175 billion parameters, GPT-3 is one of the largest language models ever created.

The primary capability of GPT-3 is language generation. It can generate coherent and contextually relevant text based on a given prompt or input. It has shown remarkable performance in various language-related tasks, such as text completion, translation, summarization, question answering, and even creative writing.

GPT-3 can understand and generate text in multiple languages and has the ability to generate human-like responses. It can exhibit a conversational style and generate contextually appropriate responses in a wide range of topics.

The model's versatility and general-purpose nature make it applicable to various domains, including content generation, virtual assistants, customer support chatbots, language translation, and more.

It is important to note that GPT-3 is a pre-trained model, which means it has been trained on a large corpus of data before being fine-tuned for specific tasks. Fine-tuning allows developers to adapt the model to perform specific tasks or exhibit desired behavior.

GPT3 Best Practices:

When working with GPT-3, here are some best practices to keep in mind:

1. Clearly define the task: By providing clear instructions and context to GPT-3, you can guide it to generate more accurate and relevant responses tailored to your specific needs.

2. Control the output: Utilize system-level and token-level prompts to influence the model's output. Experiment with different prompt strategies to achieve the desired results and ensure the generated content aligns with your intentions.

3. Iterate and refine: GPT-3 may not always produce perfect output in the initial attempts. Continuously iterate and refine your prompts and instructions to improve the quality and relevance of the generated text over time.

4. Be cautious with sensitive information: Exercise caution when sharing sensitive or confidential information with GPT-3, as it lacks the ability to guarantee privacy or security. Avoid disclosing sensitive data during interactions with the model.

5. Use temperature and max tokens: Adjust the temperature parameter to control the level of randomness in the generated output. Higher values (e.g., 0.8) lead to more creative and diverse responses, while lower values (e.g., 0.2) result in more focused and deterministic output. Additionally, set an appropriate max tokens limit to restrict the length of the generated response.

6. Understand limitations: Although GPT-3 is trained on vast amounts of text, it may still exhibit biases, factual inaccuracies, or produce content that requires human verification. Remain aware of these limitations and critically evaluate the generated text for any potential issues.

7. Ethical considerations: Employ GPT-3 responsibly and consider the ethical implications of the generated content. Avoid generating or spreading harmful or misleading information, ensuring that the output aligns with ethical guidelines and legal requirements.

8. Experiment and learn: GPT-3 is a powerful tool, and experimentation is key to unlocking its full potential. Explore various use cases, prompt styles, and techniques to gain a better understanding of its capabilities and limitations.

Section 4.4.1: GPT3 Text Models in Detail [8] :

Model Name	Model Description	GPT Version	Used For
text-davinci-003 **text-davinci-002**	It is the most capable GPT model developed by OpenAI. Can generate human-like text.	GPT3	The Davinci model is a variant of the GPT model developed by OpenAI. It is known for its impressive language generation capabilities and is often used for various natural language processing tasks, including text completion, summarization, translation, and more. The Davinci model has a large number of parameters and can generate high-quality, contextually coherent text across a wide range of topics and prompts. It is designed to provide advanced language understanding and generation capabilities for applications that require sophisticated language processing.
text-curie-001	It is a GPT model developed by OpenAI. It is specifically designed for language generation tasks and is known for its versatility and adaptability. It is capable of generating human-like text.	GPT3	The Curie model is another variant of the GPT model developed by OpenAI. It is specifically designed for language generation tasks and is known for its versatility and adaptability. Curie is trained on a diverse range of internet text, allowing it to generate coherent and contextually relevant responses. It can be used for various natural language processing applications such as chatbots, question answering systems, text completion, and more. The Curie model combines powerful language understanding capabilities with the ability to generate human-like text, making it a valuable tool for developers and researchers working on language-related tasks.

---

[8] Deprecation of the model can be found in the following links

https://platform.openai.com/docs/deprecations

Foe Azure OpenAI GPT3 and GPT 3.5 models are not available for new deployment starting July 6th 2023

Model Type[9]	Model Description	Version	**Used For**
Similarity **text-similarity-ada-001** **text-similarity-babbage-001** **text-similarity-curie-001** **text-similarity-davinci-001**	Models are good at capturing semantic similarity between two or more pieces of text.	GPT-3	**Clustering, regression**, anomaly detection, visualizatio n
Text search text-search-ada-doc-001 text-search-ada-query-001 text-search-babbage-doc-001 text-search-babbage-query-001 text-search-curie-doc-001 text-search-curie-query-001 text-search-davinci-	Support two types input doc and query	GPT-3	**Search, context relevance**, informatio n retrieval

---

[9] Deprecation of the model can be found in the following links

https://platform.openai.com/docs/deprecations

Foe Azure OpenAI GPT3 and GPT 3.5 models are not available for new deployment starting July 6th 2023

doc-001 text-search-davinci-query-001			
Code search code-search-ada-code-001 code-search-ada-text-001 code-search-babbage-code-001 code-search-babbage-text-001	Similar to the text search embedding. Use two input code & test	GPT-3	**Code search** and relevance

Best Practices for GPT3 Text Models:

Best practices for using OpenAI's text models (text-davinci-003, text-davinci-002, text-curie-001, text-babbage-001, text-ada-001) can be summarized as follows:

1. Clearly define the task: Clearly specify the desired task or prompt to ensure accurate and relevant responses from the text models. Provide specific instructions and context to guide the generated text effectively.

2. Control the output: Utilize system-level and token-level prompts to guide the model's output. Experiment with different prompt strategies to achieve desired results and ensure the generated content aligns with your intentions.

3. Iterate and refine: Continuously iterate and refine your prompts and instructions to enhance the quality and relevance of the generated text. Experiment with different approaches to optimize the model's output.

4. Validate and fact-check: While the text models strive to provide accurate information, it is essential to validate and fact-check the generated content, especially for critical or sensitive topics. Use external sources and human verification to ensure accuracy.

5. Understand limitations: Recognize that text models may have limitations such as biases or factual inaccuracies. Evaluate the generated content critically and exercise caution, particularly in sensitive or controversial subjects.

6. Ethical considerations: Utilize the text models responsibly and consider the ethical implications of the generated content. Avoid generating harmful or misleading information and ensure compliance with ethical guidelines and legal requirements.

7. Monitor and fine-tune: Continuously monitor and fine-tune your approach based on the model's performance and user feedback. Adjust prompts, instructions, and parameters to improve the model's output over time.

Example of GPT 3 Model Application

1. Content generation: OpenAI's GPT-3 model can be utilized for content generation tasks. For example, the "davinci" variant of GPT-3 is known for its ability to generate high-quality and coherent text across various topics.

2. Language translation: OpenAI's GPT-3 model can be applied for language translation tasks. By providing a source text in one language and using the "davinci" variant of GPT-3, it can generate translated text in the desired target language.

3. Virtual assistants and chatbots: GPT-3 models like "davinci" can power virtual assistants and chatbots. By fine-tuning the model and training it on specific conversational data, it can deliver more personalized and context-aware responses to user queries.

4. Tutoring and education: GPT-3 models like "davinci" can be employed as educational tools. They can provide explanations, answer questions, and assist with learning materials across various subjects, making them useful in tutoring and e-learning platforms.

5. Creative applications: OpenAI's GPT-3 models, particularly the "davinci" variant, can be used in creative applications such as generating poetry, artwork descriptions, or assisting in music composition. These models exhibit a high level of creativity and can generate unique and imaginative content in response to given prompts.

It's important to note that while GPT-3 models like "davinci" are powerful and versatile, OpenAI's models are continuously evolving, and newer models may offer even more advanced capabilities in the future.

Section 4.5: GPT 3.5 Turbo Model (gpt-35-turbo & gpt-35-turbo-16k)

GPT3.5 Turbo (Family of GPT 3.5) is an advanced language model developed by OpenAI. It is an enhanced version of the GPT-3 model, designed to generate human-like text and provide more accurate responses. GPT-3.5 Turbo has a vast understanding of various topics and can perform tasks such as language translation, question answering, text generation, and more.

Compared to its predecessor, GPT-3, the GPT-3.5 Turbo model offers similar capabilities but with improved efficiency. It is faster and more cost-effective, allowing for quicker response times and reduced resource consumption.

With its enhanced performance, GPT-3.5 Turbo is widely used in applications such as chatbots, virtual assistants, content generation, and language-related tasks that require natural language processing capabilities. It demonstrates OpenAI's continuous efforts to refine and optimize their language models to provide better user experiences and more efficient AI-powered solutions.

Its available with two models gpt-35-turbo & gpt-35-turbo-16k. Only difference between gpt-35-turbo supports max 4096 input tokens & gpt-35-turbo-16k supports max 16,384 input tokens.

Model Name	Model Description	GPT Version	Used For
ChatGPT-Model	GPT 3.5 Turbo is an advanced language model developed by OpenAI. gpt-35-turbo supports 4096 maximum input tokens	GPT3	The Davinci model is a variant of the GPT model developed by OpenAI. "GPT-3.5 Turbo" is a powerful language model used for a range of natural language processing tasks. It is commonly applied in areas such as chatbots, content generation, language translation, question answering, text summarization, sentiment analysis, and language understanding and generation. With its advanced capabilities, GPT-

gpt-35-turbo-16k supports 16,384 maximum input tokens	3.5 Turbo enables human-like interactions, text generation, language translation, and other language-related tasks. It is a versatile tool that offers valuable solutions for developers, researchers, and organizations in need of sophisticated natural language processing capabilities.

GPT 3.5 Turbo Best Practices

When working with GPT-3.5 Turbo, here are some best practices to consider:

1. Provide clear instructions: Clearly specify the desired task or objective in your prompt to guide the model's response effectively. Be explicit about the format, structure, or constraints if necessary.

2. Use system-level and token-level prompts: System-level prompts provide high-level context to guide the model's behavior throughout the conversation. Token-level prompts allow you to fine-tune the model's response by including specific instructions within the text.

3. Experiment with temperature and max tokens: Temperature controls the randomness of the output. Higher values (e.g., 0.8) result in more diverse responses, while lower values (e.g., 0.2) produce more focused and deterministic output. Max tokens limit the length of the generated response.

4. Iterate and refine your prompts: Experiment with different prompts and iterations to achieve the desired results. Refine and adjust your prompts based on the output generated by the model.

5. Verify and fact-check the generated content: While GPT-3.5 Turbo is powerful, it can sometimes generate incorrect or misleading information. It's essential to verify and fact-check the generated content before using it in critical or factual contexts.

6. Consider ethical implications: Be mindful of the ethical considerations when using GPT-3.5 Turbo. Avoid generating content that promotes hate speech, misinformation, or violates ethical guidelines. Use the model responsibly and ensure compliance with relevant laws and regulations.

7. Understand the limitations of the model: GPT-3.5 Turbo, like any AI model, has its limitations. It may not always provide accurate answers, and it's important to be aware of its strengths and weaknesses. Avoid over-reliance on the model and supplement its output with human judgment and expertise when necessary.

8. Continually monitor and adapt your approach: Keep track of the model's performance, gather user feedback, and adapt your approach accordingly. Fine-tune your prompts, adjust parameters, and incorporate user feedback to improve the quality and effectiveness of the generated content.

GPT 35 Turbo Application:

These are just a few examples of the diverse range of applications where GPT-3.5 Turbo can be utilized to enhance productivity, enable language processing tasks, and support creative endeavors.

1. Content Generation: GPT-3.5 Turbo can be used to generate various types of content, such as articles, blog posts, social media captions, and product descriptions. It can assist in creating engaging and informative written material.

2. Language Translation: GPT-3.5 Turbo can be employed for language translation tasks. It can help translate text from one language to another, facilitating communication and understanding across language barriers.

3. Code Generation: GPT-3.5 Turbo has the ability to generate code in multiple programming languages. It can assist developers by automatically generating code snippets, functions, or even entire programs based on provided prompts and requirements.

4. Virtual Assistants and Chatbots: GPT-3.5 Turbo can be used to create virtual assistants and chatbots that engage in conversational interactions with users. It can understand and respond to user queries, provide information, and offer assistance in a conversational manner.

5. Creative Writing and Storytelling: GPT-3.5 Turbo can be harnessed for creative writing purposes, such as generating poems, stories, or scripts. It can assist authors, writers, and content creators in generating imaginative and engaging content.

Section 4.6 Difference Between GPT3 and GPT 35 Turbo

Model	GPT-3	ChatGPT-Turbo
Description	Powerful language model capable of various NLP tasks	Language model optimized specifically for chat-based interactions
Use Cases	Content generation, translation, question answering, summarization, sentiment analysis, etc.	Chatbot development, customer support, conversational AI
Performance	Higher performance with large-scale language tasks	Optimized for chat-based tasks, provides similar capabilities with faster response times
Type	Text in - Text Out	Message-In -Message-Out
Example	Question: "What is the capital of France?"Answer: "Paris"	Chatbot interaction: User: "What's the weather like today?" ChatGPT-Turbo: "The weather today is sunny with a high of 25 degrees Celsius.

Section 4.7: GPT-3 -Codex

Codex is an advanced AI model created by OpenAI specifically designed to convert natural language into code. It has the capability to comprehend general natural language descriptions and generate corresponding code. As the successor to the GPT series, Codex has been extensively trained on a vast dataset of code sourced from GitHub. It excels in generating code in various programming languages such as C#, JavaScript, Go, Perl, PHP, Ruby, Swift, TypeScript, SQL, and Shell. With its powerful capabilities, Codex revolutionizes the process of programming by providing an efficient and intuitive way to translate language into functional code.

Codex is particularly adept at assisting with programming tasks, such as generating code snippets, providing code completion suggestions, and even translating natural language descriptions into functional code. It can be used in various software development scenarios, such as writing scripts, automating repetitive tasks, and assisting developers in finding solutions to coding challenges.

One of the prominent features of Codex is its ability to understand context and generate code that aligns with the developer's intent. It can work with multiple programming languages and libraries, making it a versatile tool for programmers working on diverse projects. Codex is often integrated into Integrated Development Environments (IDEs) or used through APIs to provide developers with intelligent code generation capabilities.

4.7.1 Codex Model [10]

Model Name	Model Description	GPT Version	Used For
code-davinci-002	Compared to other models like GPT-3 Davinci and Codex Davinci, this advanced model outperforms them by requiring less instruction while delivering superior performance. However, it is important to note that this model is associated with a higher cost due to its exceptional capabilities.	GPT-3 [9]	Codex convert the natural language to code
code-cushman-001	It is less powerful, and cost less as compared to the Codex Davinci	GPT-3	Codex convert the natural language to code

Best Practices for Codex:

1. Clearly define the coding task: Clearly specify the desired coding task or function you want GPT-3 Codex to generate. Provide specific instructions, input-output examples, and context to guide the model in producing accurate and relevant code.

2. Incremental refinement: Iterate and refine your prompts and instructions to improve the quality and accuracy of the generated code. Start with small code snippets and gradually

---

[10] **Note:** Some of the model may be deprecated or due for deprecation for more information : Deprecation of the model can be found in the following links https://platform.openai.com/docs/deprecations
Foe Azure OpenAI GPT3 and GPT 3.5 models are not available for new deployment starting July 6th 2023

increase complexity, ensuring the model's output aligns with your coding requirements.

3. Validate and test: Always verify the generated code by testing and validating its functionality. Review the code for correctness, efficiency, and security considerations. Use human code review and testing methodologies to ensure the reliability and safety of the generated code.

Application of Codex Examples:

1. **Code generation:** Codex can be used to generate code snippets or entire programs based on natural language descriptions or requirements. It can assist developers in automating repetitive coding tasks, prototyping new functionality, or generating code templates.

2. **Documentation generation: Codex** can be utilized to generate documentation for codebases. By providing a description or query about a specific code component, Codex can generate clear and concise documentation, helping developers understand the code and its functionality.

3. **Code completion and suggestions:** Codex can offer code completion suggestions while developers are writing code. It can understand the context and provide relevant code snippets,

function signatures, or variable names to speed up the coding process and enhance productivity.

4. Bug fixing and error resolution: Codex can assist in debugging and error resolution by analyzing code snippets or error messages and providing possible solutions or insights into the cause of the issue. It can help developers identify and fix bugs more efficiently.

5. Code translation and adaptation: Codex has the ability to translate code between different programming languages. It can help in porting codebases to new languages, adapting code from one language to another, or providing syntax conversions between different programming paradigms.

Example Codex:

Example 1 :	Result :
#Convert the SQL Code to Spark 3.0 Sql _ code = '''CREATE TABLE customers (id INT PRIMARY KEY, name VARCHAR(50), email VARCHAR(100), address VARCHAR(200), phone VARCHAR(20));''' print the code	from pyspark.sql import SparkSession from pyspark.sql.types import * spark = SparkSession.builder.appName('SparkByExamples.com').getOrCreate() schema = StructType([StructField("id", IntegerType(), True), StructField("name", StringType(), True), StructField("email", StringType(), True), StructField("address", StringType(),

SUMMARY & CONCLUSION- CODEX

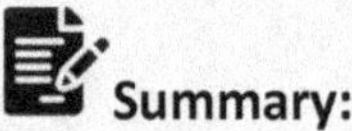 **Summary:**

Codex:

Codex is an advanced AI model developed by OpenAI that can convert natural language into functional code. It's designed to assist developers in generating code snippets, scripts, and more. Codex's capabilities can greatly accelerate software development and automation tasks by translating human language instructions into executable code their ability to understand and process textual data effectively

Section 4.8: GPT3-Embedding

Embedding refers to the process of representing words, phrases, or even entire sentences as numerical vectors in a multi-dimensional space. These vectors capture semantic relationships between words, making it possible for machine learning models to understand and process textual data. Embeddings are often used as inputs to various natural language processing (NLP) tasks, such as sentiment analysis, machine translation, and document clustering

GPT-3, or Generative Pre-trained Transformer 3, is a powerful language model developed by OpenAI. While GPT-3 is primarily known for its text generation capabilities, it can also be used for text embedding.

In the context of GPT-3, embedding refers to the process of representing words, sentences, or documents as dense numerical vectors. GPT-3 is trained on a large corpus of text data and learns to encode the semantic meaning and contextual relationships between different pieces of text.

With GPT-3, you can input a piece of text, such as a word, sentence, or paragraph, and the model will generate an embedding that represents the meaning and context of that text. These embeddings can then be used for various natural language processing tasks, including sentiment analysis, text classification, semantic similarity, and more.

The advantage of using GPT-3 for embedding is that it captures complex language patterns and context due to its large-scale pre-training on diverse text sources. However, it's important to note that GPT-3's primary strength lies in text generation rather than embedding, and there are other models specifically designed for text embedding tasks that may offer more optimized performance in that regard.

Example of Word Embedding:

Consider the words "king," "queen," "man," and "woman." In a word embedding space, these words might have numerical vectors like:

- "king": [0.2, 0.5, -0.3]

- "queen": [0.1, 0.6, -0.4]

- "man": [0.3, 0.4, -0.2]

- "woman": [0.2, 0.7, -0.1]

In this hypothetical example, the vectors for "king" and "queen" are close to each other, indicating a gender relationship. Similarly, the vectors for "man" and "woman" are close, indicating another gender relationship.

Word embeddings capture semantic relationships even for words that are not directly related. For instance, in the embedding space, the vector calculation "queen" - "woman" + "man" might result in a vector very close to "king," illustrating that "queen" is to "woman" as "king" is to "man."

Section 4.9 Compare GPT3 and GPT3 -Embedding:

Parameters	GPT-3[9]	GPT-3 Embedding[10]
Purpose	Natural language processing and generation	Embedding text into fixed-length numerical vectors
Function	Generates human-like text based on prompts	Converts text into dense vector representations

Comparison:

Parameters	GPT-3[11]	GPT-3 Embedding[12]
Purpose	Natural language processing and generation	Embedding text into fixed-length numerical vectors
Function	Generates human-like text based on prompts	Converts text into dense vector representations
Input	Text prompts	Text inputs for embedding
Output	**Generated text**	**Embeddings (numerical vectors)**
Training Data	Diverse range of sources (web pages, books, etc.)	N/A (No explicit training on embedding)
Usage	Language génération, chat bots, content création, etc.	Semantic similarity, clustering, information retrieval, etc.
Flexibility	More flexible for generating diverse text outputs	Less flexible as it focuses on embedding tasks
Cost	Varies based on usage and API pricing	Varies based on usage and API pricing
Examples	"Translate English to French: Hello, how are you?"	"Calculate the similarity between two sentences: 'I like cats' and 'I love dogs'"

---

[11] openai.com/research/gpt-3/ **Note:** Some of the model may be deprecated or due for deprecation for more information : Deprecation of the model can be found in the following links https://platform.openai.com/docs/deprecations

[12] https://platform.openai.com/docs/guides/embeddings

Section 4.10 While Working with Embedding Following things to Consider:

1. Proper input formatting: When using the embedding model in GPT-3, it is important to provide the input text in a structured and meaningful way. Ensure that the text is properly tokenized and organized to capture the desired context accurately.

2. Contextual embeddings: Utilize the contextual embeddings provided by GPT-3 to capture the meaning and relationships within the text. These embeddings can be helpful in tasks such as sentiment analysis, document classification, or information retrieval.

3. Fine-tuning: Consider fine-tuning the embedding model on specific domain-specific or task-specific data to enhance its performance for particular applications. Fine-tuning allows the model to learn more specific patterns and representations relevant to the target task.

4. Handling out-of-vocabulary (OOV) words: GPT-3's embedding model may encounter out-of-vocabulary words that are not present in its training data. Implement proper strategies to handle OOV words, such as using word embeddings from external sources or employing contextual approximation methods.

5. Evaluation and validation: Thoroughly evaluate and validate the performance of the embedding model for the intended task. Use appropriate evaluation metrics and test it on diverse datasets to ensure its generalization and accuracy.

6. Consider model limitations: Understand the limitations of the embedding model, such as bias in language representations or limitations in capturing specific nuances. Be aware of these limitations and employ appropriate techniques to mitigate any negative impact they may have on the application.

Remember to experiment, iterate, and evaluate the performance of the embedding model based on the specific requirements and use cases to optimize its effectiveness.

Examples of Embedding

OpenAI's embedding models have diverse applications in natural language processing tasks:

1. Sentiment Analysis: Analyzing the sentiment expressed in text, such as classifying it as positive, negative, or neutral.

2. Named Entity Recognition: Identifying and classifying named entities like people, organizations, and locations in text.

3. Document Classification: Assigning predefined categories or labels to documents based on their content.

4. Text Similarity/Clustering: Measuring the similarity between texts or clustering related documents based on their semantic similarities.

Best Practices Embedding

Best practices for using embeddings effectively depend on the specific context and task you're working on. However, here are some general guidelines that can help you make the most of embeddings:

1. Choose the Right Embedding Model: Different embedding methods work better for different types of data. Word2Vec, GloVe, fastText, and BERT embeddings, for instance, have different strengths. Choose the model that aligns with your data and task requirements.

2. Pre-trained vs. Custom Embeddings: Consider whether to use pre-trained embeddings or train your own. Pre-trained embeddings are useful for many tasks, but fine-tuning or training custom embeddings can be beneficial for domain-specific data.

3. Dimensionality Embeddings often have a predefined dimensionality. Choose a dimensionality that balances between capturing nuanced features and avoiding overfitting.

4. Normalization: Normalize embeddings to unit length. This helps in improving their interpretability and comparison.

5. Embedding Visualization: Visualize embeddings using techniques like t-SNE or PCA to understand the relationships between data points.

6. Contextual Embeddings: For tasks like NLP, consider using contextual embeddings like BERT or GPT, which capture contextual information around each word.

7. Transfer Learning: Transfer learned embeddings from one task to another, especially if they are related. For instance, embeddings learned from language translation tasks can be useful for sentiment analysis.

8. Fine-Tuning: If using pre-trained embeddings, you might need to fine-tune them for your specific task to capture domain-specific information.

9 Data Quality High-quality training data leads to better embeddings. Ensure your training data is diverse, relevant, and representative of your target task.

10. Regularization: Apply regularization techniques like dropout to prevent overfitting when training custom embeddings.

SUMMARY & CONCLUSION- EMBEDDING

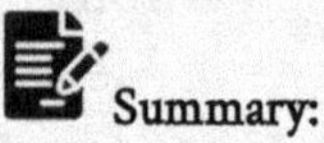 **Summary:**

1. **Embedding:** Embedding is a technique to convert words or text into numerical vectors, preserving semantic relationships. These vectors are used as inputs for machine learning models, enhancing their ability to understand and process textual data effectively.

SUMMARY & CONCLUSION GPT3 Model

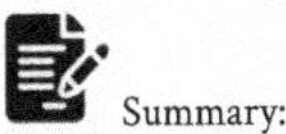 Summary:

The GPT-3 text model, along with its various versions such as Davinci, Curie, Babbage, Ada, Davinci Codex, and Cushman Codex, provides a range of capabilities for language processing tasks. GPT-3.5 Turbo combines efficiency and power, offering enhanced performance and cost-effectiveness. Embeddings play a crucial role in representing and analyzing text, enabling advanced natural language processing tasks.

GPT-3 models, including Davinci, Curie, Babbage, and Ada, have different token counts and applications. Davinci is the most capable but expensive and slower, while Curie, Babbage, and Ada offer options for specific tasks and costs. The Davinci Codex excels in converting natural language to code, while Cushman Codex provides a more affordable alternative.

The concept of embeddings provides a mathematical representation of words or sentences, capturing their semantic meaning. This technique is instrumental in performing various natural language processing tasks, such as language translation and sentiment analysis.

Conclusion: The GPT-3 text models, along with GPT-3.5 Turbo, embeddings, and Codex models, offer a diverse set of tools for language processing. Understanding the capabilities, token counts, and costs of these models is crucial in selecting the most suitable option for specific tasks and budget constraints.

With the availability of GPT-3.5 Turbo and the power of embeddings, developers and organizations have access to more efficient and powerful language processing capabilities. These advancements contribute to the automation of language-related tasks, driving innovation in industries such as content generation, translation, question answering, code conversion, and more.

As the field of natural language processing continues to evolve, models like GPT-3 and techniques like embeddings play a vital role in advancing language understanding and automation. Leveraging these tools responsibly and ethically can lead to transformative applications in various domains, improving efficiency, accuracy, and accessibility in language-related tasks.

Note All the models in the OpenAI are available in Azure OpenAI and Azure Cloud infrastructure are enterprise grade compliance are available in the Azure OpenAI.

CHAPTER 4 QUIZ: GPT MODELS

1. What is the token capacity of the Davinci model?

    a) 2048

    b) 3072

    c) 4096

    d) 5120

2. What are some applications of the Curie model?

    a) Machine translation

    b) Chatbots

    c) Image recognition

    d) Speech synthesis

3. How does the cost of the Babbage model compare to the other models?

    a) Most expensive

    b) Least expensive

    c) Moderate cost

    d) No cost

4. What tasks is the Ada model suitable for?

    a) Natural language processing

    b) Sentiment analysis

    c) Computer vision

    d) Reinforcement learning

5. What is the main capability of the Davinci Codex model?

    a) Speech recognition

    b) Image generation

    c) Code conversion

    d) Language translation

6. How does the power of the Cushman Codex model compare to the Davinci model?

    a) More powerful

    b) Less powerful

    c) Equally powerful

    d) Depends on the task

7. Which model is recommended for complex intent and summarization for audience?

    a) Curie

    b) Babbage

    c) Davinci

d) Ada

8. Which model is more affordable compared to Davinci but more powerful than Ada?

a) Babbage

b) Curie

c) Davinci Codex

d) Cushman Codex

9. What tasks is the Babbage model commonly used for?

a) Image recognition

b) Sentiment analysis

c) Semantic search

d) Speech synthesis

10. Which model is the least expensive but also less powerful than the other models?

a) Davinci Codex

b) Cushman Codex

c) Babbage

d) Ada

CHAPTER 4 QUIZ: GPT MODEL ANSWERS

1. What is the token capacity of the Davinci model?

    Answer: c) 4096

2. What are some applications of the Curie model?

    Answer: b) Chatbots

3. How does the cost of the Babbage model compare to the other models?

    Answer: c) Moderate cost

4. What tasks is the Ada model suitable for?

    Answer: a) Natural language processing

5. What is the main capability of the Davinci Codex model?

    Answer: c) Code conversion

6. How does the power of the Cushman Codex model compare to the Davinci model?

    Answer: b) Less powerful

7. Which model is recommended for complex intent and summarization for audience?

    Answer: c) Davinci

8. Which model is more affordable compared to Davinci but more powerful than Ada?

    Answer: a) Babbage

9. What tasks is the Babbage model commonly used for?

Answer: c) Semantic search

10. Which model is the least expensive but also less powerful than the other models?

Answer: d) Ada

CHAPTER 4 QUIZ:
GPT-3.5 Turbo, Embedding, and Codex

1. What is the maximum token limit for GPT-3.5 Turbo?

   a) 2048 tokens

   b) 4096 tokens

   c) 8192 tokens

   d) 1024 tokens

2. How does the Embedding model differ from GPT-3.5 Turbo in terms of its primary application?

   a) Embedding is specialized for natural language understanding.

   b) Embedding is designed for code generation tasks.

   c) Embedding focuses on machine translation.

   d) Embedding is optimized for text summarization.

3. What are some common use cases for the Codex model?

   a) Sentiment analysis and sentiment classification.

   b) Image recognition and object detection.

   c) Speech-to-text conversion and voice recognition.

d) Natural language to code conversion and programming assistance.

4. How does the power of GPT-3.5 Turbo compare to GPT-3?

a) GPT-3.5 Turbo is less powerful than GPT-3.

b) GPT-3.5 Turbo has the same level of power as GPT-3.

c) GPT-3.5 Turbo is more powerful than GPT-3.

d) GPT-3.5 Turbo has a completely different power scale than GPT-3.

5. What is the main advantage of using the Embedding model for text processing tasks?

a) Fast processing speed and low computational cost.

b) High accuracy and precision in natural language understanding.

c) Ability to handle large-scale datasets and complex patterns.

d) Seamless integration with other machine learning models and frameworks.

6. Can GPT-3.5 Turbo generate code snippets or only text-based responses?

a) GPT-3.5 Turbo can only generate text-based responses.

b) GPT-3.5 Turbo can generate both code snippets and text-based responses.

c) GPT-3.5 Turbo is specialized for code generation tasks only.

d) GPT-3.5 Turbo is unable to generate any kind of code.

7. How does the cost of using the Codex model compare to GPT-3.5 Turbo?

a) Codex is more expensive than GPT-3.5 Turbo.

b) Codex is less expensive than GPT-3.5 Turbo.

c) Codex and GPT-3.5 Turbo have similar pricing.

d) The cost varies depending on the specific use case and requirements.

8. In what scenarios would you choose to use GPT-3.5 Turbo over the Embedding model?

a) When performing sentiment analysis and text classification tasks.

b) When focusing on code generation and programming assistance.

c) When dealing with image recognition and computer vision tasks.

d) When prioritizing natural language understanding and comprehension.

9. What are the key capabilities of the GPT-3.5 Turbo model?

a) Advanced speech recognition and voice synthesis.

b) Robust text summarization and content generation.

c) Real-time natural language translation and multilingual support.

d) Accurate sentiment analysis and emotion detection.

10. Can the Embedding model be used for both text classification and semantic search tasks?

a) Yes, the Embedding model is suitable for both tasks.

b) No, the Embedding model is specialized only for text classification.

c) No, the Embedding model is specialized only for semantic search.

d) Yes, but it is

SPECIAL QUIZ

Section #1 Embedding

1. What is the purpose of text embedding?

a) Converting text to images

b) Transforming text into numerical vectors

c) Generating summaries of text

d) Translating text into multiple languages

2. Which of the following is a common technique for word embedding?

a) OCR (Optical Character Recognition)

b) BERT (Bidirectional Encoder Representations from Transformers)

c) GPS (Global Positioning System)

d) CD-ROM (Compact Disc Read-Only Memory)

Section #2 Codex

1. What is the primary function of Codex, developed by OpenAI?

a) Generating images from text descriptions

b) Translating languages in real-time

c) Assisting with code generation and understanding

d) Providing weather forecasts

2. How does Codex understand programming languages and generate code?

a) It uses pre-written code templates

b) It analyzes syntax errors in existing code

c) It has been trained on a diverse range of code samples

d) It relies on manual input from developers

3. What type of development tasks can Codex assist with?

a) Cooking recipes

b) Building physical structures

c) Writing code and scripts

d) Playing musical instruments

4. What should developers keep in mind when using Codex-generated code?

a) No need to review the code, it's always accurate

b) Always test the generated code thoroughly

c) Use Codex for critical production code without verification

d) Use Codex for personal projects only

5. How can developers ensure the security of code generated by Codex?

a) Avoid using Codex for security-sensitive projects

b) Rely solely on Codex for code security

c) Share all generated code publicly

d) Add vulnerabilities intentionally for testing purposes

CHAPTER 4 QUIZ: ANSWERS:

1. What is the maximum token limit for GPT-3.5 Turbo?

Answer: a) 2048 tokens

2. How does the Embedding model differ from GPT-3.5 Turbo in terms of its primary application?

Answer: a) Embedding is specialized for natural language understanding.

3. What are some common use cases for the Codex model?

Answer: d) Natural language to code conversion and programming assistance.

4. How does the power of GPT-3.5 Turbo compare to GPT-3?

Answer: c) GPT-3.5 Turbo is more powerful than GPT-3.

5. What is the main advantage of using the Embedding model for text processing tasks?

Answer: a) Fast processing speed and low computational cost.

6. Can GPT-3.5 Turbo generate code snippets or only text-based responses?

Answer: b) GPT-3.5 Turbo can generate both code snippets and text-based responses.

7. How does the cost of using the Codex model compare to GPT-3.5 Turbo?

Answer: a) Codex is more expensive than GPT-3.5 Turbo.

8. In what scenarios would you choose to use GPT-3.5 Turbo over the Embedding model?

Answer: b) When focusing on code generation and programming assistance.

9. What are the key capabilities of the GPT-3.5 Turbo model?

Answer: b) Robust text summarization and content generation.

10. Can the Embedding model be used for both text classification and semantic search tasks?

Answer: a) Yes, the Embedding model is suitable for both tasks.

SPECIAL QUIZ:

Section #1 Embedding

1. b) Transforming text into numerical vectors

2. b) BERT (Bidirectional Encoder Representations from Transformers)

Section #2 Codex

1 Answer: c) Assisting with code generation and understanding

2. Answer: c) It has been trained on a diverse range of code samples

3. Answer: c) Writing code and scripts

4. Answer: b) Always test the generated code thoroughly

5. Answer: a) Avoid using Codex for security-sensitive projects

Section 4.11 What is GPT4

GPT-4 is an advanced language model that has been trained on a large dataset of text and code, giving it a vast knowledge base. It demonstrates high accuracy in text generation, translation, and informative responses. Being multimodal, GPT-4 can understand and process text, images, and audio, making it versatile. The model is also steerable, allowing users to control its output through prompts and instructions. Although still under development, GPT-4 has the potential to revolutionize computer interaction, enabling new forms of creative content generation, improving machine translation, and enhancing accessibility to information. It is a promising tool with various applications.

GPT-4 offers several notable features:

1. Extensive dataset: GPT-4 has been trained on a vast collection of text and code, encompassing various sources like books, articles, and code repositories. This extensive dataset

provides GPT-4 with a wealth of knowledge for generating text and answering questions effectively.

2. High accuracy: GPT-4 exhibits remarkable accuracy in generating text and performing translations. It excels in providing informative and reliable responses.

3. Multimodal capabilities: GPT-4 is capable of understanding and processing not only text but also images and audio. This multimodal capability enhances its versatility, making it a more powerful language model compared to its predecessors.

4. User control: GPT-4 is designed to be steerable, enabling users to influence its output by supplying different prompts and instructions. This allows for greater customization and fine-tuning of the model's responses.

GPT-4's incorporation of a large dataset, high accuracy, multimodality, and user control contribute to its advanced capabilities as a language model.

GPT-4 holds significant potential in various applications:

1. Creative content generation: GPT-4 can be utilized to generate diverse forms of creative content, including poems, stories, scripts, and marketing copy like product descriptions and blog posts. Its advanced language generation abilities open avenues for automated content creation.

2. Enhanced machine translation: GPT-4 can contribute to improving the accuracy of machine translation systems. By leveraging its extensive language understanding and generation capabilities, it can aid in bridging communication gaps across different languages, facilitating smoother multilingual interactions.

3. Accessibility enhancement: GPT-4 can play a role in making information more accessible to individuals with disabilities. For instance, it can generate textual descriptions of images or videos, enabling people who are blind or visually impaired to access visual content through text-based formats.

The versatile nature of GPT-4 allows for its application in various domains, enabling automated content generation, advancing translation accuracy, and enhancing accessibility for a wider range of users.

Section 4.11.1 GPT4 Models:

Model Name	Model Description	GPT Version	Use For
GPT-4	Compared to OpenAI's previous models, GPT-4 (preview) exhibits enhanced problem-solving capabilities with improved	GPT-4	GPT-4 excels in chat functionality optimization while also delivering impressive performance in traditional completion tasks.

	accuracy. Similar to GPT-3.5-turbo, GPT-4 is optimized for chat functionality, while also demonstrating excellent performance in traditional completion tasks.	94	
gpt-4	The gpt-4 supports 8192 max input tokens the gpt-4-32k supports up to 32,768 tokens.	GPT-4	GPT-4 is specifically designed to excel in chat functionality, while also demonstrating exceptional performance in traditional completion tasks.
gpt-4-32k	the gpt-4-32k supports up to 32,768 tokens.	GPT-4	GPT-4 has been fine-tuned to deliver outstanding performance in chat-based interactions, prioritizing optimal chat functionality. Additionally, it showcases impressive capabilities in handling traditional completion tasks with remarkable proficiency.

Section 4.11.2: What is GPT -4 and Difference as compared to GPT-3

GPT-3 and GPT-4 are both powerful AI language models, but they have some key differences. Here are some of the differences between GPT-4 and GPT-3: GPT-4 is a large language model (LLM) developed by OpenAI. It is significantly larger and more powerful than previous GPT models, and it can take both text and images as input. This allows it to perform a wider range of tasks, such as generating text, answering questions, summarizing text, translating languages, and writing different kinds of creative content.

GPT-4 is still under development, but it has already demonstrated some impressive capabilities. For example, it has been shown to be able to pass a simulated bar exam with a score in the top 10% of test takers. It has also been shown to be able to generate text that is indistinguishable from human-written text.

GPT-4 has the potential to be used in a wide variety of applications, both good and bad. It could be used to improve the quality of customer service, generate creative content, or even help people with disabilities. However, it is also possible that GPT-4 could be used to generate harmful or offensive content, or to create deepfakes.

It is important to use GPT-4 responsibly and ethically. With its powerful capabilities, it is a tool that could be used for great good or great harm. It is up to us to ensure that it is used for the former.

Here are some of the new features of GPT-4:

- It is larger and more powerful than previous GPT models.

- It is multimodal, meaning it can take both text and images as input.

- It is more aligned with human ethics.

- It is more steerable, meaning it can be changed its behavior according to user requests.

GPT-4 is still under development, but it has the potential to revolutionize the field of artificial intelligence. It is a powerful tool that has the potential to be used for good or evil. It is important to use it responsibly and ethically.

GPT4 Summary:

1. **Dataset Size:** GPT-4 has a significantly larger dataset compared to GPT-3. This enables GPT-4 to learn more about the world and generate more accurate text.[13]

---

[13] GPT-4: OpenAI's Next-Generation Language Model: https://openai.com/blog/openai-api/

2. **Parameters:** Both GPT-4 and GPT-3 have the same number of parameters. However, GPT-4 utilizes them more efficiently due to an improved training method.[14]

3. **Training Method:** Both GPT-4 and GPT-3 employ self-supervised learning. However, GPT-4 is trained on a larger dataset and utilizes a more advanced training method.[15]

4. **Accuracy: GPT-4** exhibits significantly higher accuracy compared to GPT-3. It is less likely to generate incorrect or misleading text.[16]

5. **Factual Correctness:** GPT-4 excels in generating factually correct text that aligns with known facts, minimizing the chance of producing false or misleading information.[17]

---

[14] GPT-4: OpenAI's Next-Generation Language Model: https://openai.com/blog/openai-api/

[15] GPT-4: OpenAI's Next-Generation Language Model: https://openai.com/blog/openai-api/

[16] GPT-4 vs. GPT-3: How Much Difference Is There?: https://www.digitaltrends.com/computing/gpt-4-vs-gpt-35/

[17] GPT-4 vs. GPT-3: How Much Difference Is There?: https://www.digitaltrends.com/computing/gpt-4-vs-gpt-35/

6. **Steerability:** GPT-4 is highly steerable, allowing users to control its output by providing specific prompts and instructions.[18]

7. **Multimodality:** GPT-4 is a multimodal model capable of understanding and processing text, images, and audio. This versatility enhances its capabilities compared to GPT-3.[19]

8. **Availability:** While GPT-3 was limited to a select number of users, GPT-4 is available in public beta. This wider availability allows more users to utilize GPT-4 for tasks like text generation, language translation, content creation, and informative responses.[20]

---

[18] GPT-4 vs. GPT-3: How Much Difference Is There?:
https://www.digitaltrends.com/computing/gpt-4-vs-gpt-35/
[19] GPT-4: OpenAI's Next-Generation Language Model: https://openai.com/blog/openai-api/
[20] OpenAI API: https://openai.com/api/

GPT-3[21]	GPT-4[22]
Unsupervised learning model	Supervised learning model
Pre-trained	First version of GPT to feature a hybrid training system
Capable of generating longer and more complex text than GPT-3	Can generate even longer and more complex text than GPT-3
Model size is 175 billion parameters	Model size is expected to be 1 trillion parameters
Can handle conversations more profoundly and answer with increased accuracy	Can handle images as inputs
Factual correctness good	Factual correctness excellent
No multi-modality	Have Multi-modality

---

[21] GPT-4 vs. GPT-3: How Much Difference Is There?:
https://www.digitaltrends.com/computing/gpt-4-vs-gpt-35/
[22] GPT-4 vs. GPT-3: How Much Difference Is There?:
https://www.digitaltrends.com/computing/gpt-4-vs-gpt-35/

SUMMARY & CONCLUSION GPT4 – GPT3

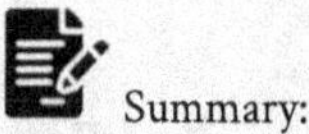 Summary:

GPT-4 is an advanced language model that exhibits high accuracy in text generation, translation, and informative responses. It has been trained on a large dataset of text and code, making it knowledgeable and versatile. GPT-4 is multimodal, capable of understanding and processing text, images, and audio, and offers user control for customized outputs. It has the potential to revolutionize computer interaction, content generation, machine translation, and accessibility to information.

 **Conclusion:**

GPT-4 represents a significant advancement in language models, with its larger dataset, improved accuracy, multimodal capabilities, and user control. It offers various applications in automated content generation, translation accuracy improvement, and accessibility enhancement. However, as with any powerful tool, responsible and ethical use of GPT-4 is crucial. Its potential for both positive and negative impact necessitates careful consideration and vigilance in ensuring its use for beneficial purposes.

In conclusion, both OpenAI and Azure OpenAI offer valuable resources and capabilities for AI development. OpenAI focuses on AI research and models, while Azure OpenAI provides a comprehensive cloud platform with additional features and services. By considering the specific needs of your project, you can make an informed decision on which option is best suited for your AI endeavors.

Note All the models in the OpenAI are available in Azure OpenAI and Azure Cloud infrastructure are enterprise grade compliance are available in the Azure OpenAI.

CHAPTER 4 QUIZ: GPT-4 and GPT-3

1. Which language model has a larger dataset for training?

   a) GPT-4

   b) GPT-3

   c) Both have the same dataset size

   d) It is not specified

2. Which language model is more accurate in generating text?

   a) GPT-4

   b) GPT-3

   c) Both have similar accuracy levels

   d) It is not specified

3. Which language model is more steerable in terms of output control?

   a) GPT-4

   b) GPT-3

   c) Both have similar steerability

   d) It is not specified

4. Which language model is multimodal, capable of understanding and processing text, images, and audio?

    a) GPT-4

    b) GPT-3

    c) Both are multimodal

    d) It is not specified

5. Which language model is more widely available for public use?

    a) GPT-4

    b) GPT-3

    c) Both have limited availability

    d) It is not specified

6. Which language model has a larger number of parameters?

    a) GPT-4

    b) GPT-3

    c) Both have the same number of parameters

    d) It is not specified

Please note that these questions are hypothetical, and the actual specifications and capabilities of GPT-4 may differ from what is mentioned here.

CHAPTER 4 QUIZ: GPT-4 and GPT-3 ANSWER

1. Which language model has a larger dataset for training?

   Answer: GPT4

2. Which language model is more accurate in generating text?

   Answer: GPT4

3. Which language model is more steerable in terms of output control?

   Answer: GPT4

4. Which language model is multimodal, capable of understanding and processing text, images, and audio?

   Answer: GPT4

5. Which language model is more widely available for public use?

   Answer: GPT3

6. Which language model has a larger number of parameters?

   Answer: GPT4

Chapter 5

How do tokens work in GPT models

Section 5.1: How do tokens work in GPT models

In GPT, a token is a basic unit of text that is used to process and generate language. Tokens can represent individual characters, words, or sub words depending on the specific tokenization approach. By breaking down text into tokens, GPT models can effectively analyze and generate coherent and contextually appropriate responses.

Here are some examples of tokens:

- In character-level tokenization, each individual character becomes a token. For example, the sentence "Hello, world!" would be tokenized into the following tokens: ['H', 'e', 'l', 'l', 'o', ',', ' ', 'w', 'o', 'r', 'l', 'd', '! '].

- In word-level tokenization, each word becomes a token. For example, the sentence "Hello, world!" would be tokenized into the following tokens: ['hello', 'world', '!'].

- In sub word tokenization, words are broken down into smaller sub words. For example, the word "hello" would be tokenized into the following sub words: ['hel', 'lo'].

The specific tokenization approach that is used can affect the performance of a GPT model. For example, character-level tokenization is typically less efficient than word-level or sub word tokenization, but it can be more accurate in certain cases.

The number of tokens in a piece of text is often used as a measure of its length. For example, a sentence with 10 words would typically have about 10 tokens. However, the number of tokens can vary depending on the tokenization approach that is used.

The token limit in GPT-3 is 4,000 tokens (approximately 3,000 words) including input and output. This means that a GPT-3 model can only generate a response that is up to 4,000 tokens long. If a response is longer than 4,000 tokens, the model will truncate it.

The token limit in GPT-3 is designed to prevent the model from consuming too much memory and processing time. It also helps to ensure that the model's responses are coherent and relevant.

Section 5.2: Key benefits of using Azure OpenAI as a developer

Here are some of the key benefits of using Azure OpenAI as a developer:

Access to powerful language models: Azure OpenAI provides access to OpenAI's powerful language models, including GPT-3, Codex, and DALL-E. These models can be used for a variety of tasks, such as generating text, translating languages, writing different kinds of creative content, and answering your questions in an informative way.

Enterprise-grade security: Azure OpenAI is built on the same security foundation as Microsoft Azure, which means that your data is protected from unauthorized access. Azure OpenAI also offers a variety of security features, such as private networking and content filtering, to help you protect your applications.

Scalability: Azure OpenAI is designed to scale to meet the needs of your applications. You can easily increase or decrease the number of instances of Azure OpenAI that you use, depending on your traffic levels.

Ease of use: Azure OpenAI is easy to use, even if you are not a machine learning expert. You can use the Azure OpenAI REST API, Python SDK, or web-based interface to interact with the service.

Community support: Azure OpenAI has a large and active community of developers who are willing to help you get started and troubleshoot problems.

Overall, Azure OpenAI is a powerful and versatile language model service that can be used to build a wide variety of applications. If you are a developer looking for a reliable and secure language model service, then Azure OpenAI is a great option.

Examples of use cases where Azure OpenAI has been successfully implemented

Use Cases and Examples of GPT Models in Various Industries

1. GPT models have found extensive applications across various industries, revolutionizing the way businesses interact with customers and automate processes. Here are a few examples:

2. **Customer Support:** GPT models can be deployed as virtual assistants or chatbots to handle customer

inquiries and provide instant support. They can understand customer queries, provide relevant information, and even troubleshoot common issues. For instance, a GPT-powered chatbot can assist customers in finding products, provide recommendations, and address frequently asked questions.

3. **Content Generation:** GPT models excel in generating high-quality content for various purposes. They can help writers and content creators by generating blog posts, articles, product descriptions, and social media captions. GPT models can also assist in creative writing tasks, such as generating storylines, dialogues, and poetry.

4. **Chatbot Development:** GPT models are widely used in developing intelligent chatbots that can engage in human-like conversations. These chatbots can understand user queries, provide relevant responses, and offer personalized recommendations. They can simulate natural conversations, making interactions with chatbots more engaging and satisfying.

5. **Language Translation:** GPT models have shown promising results in machine translation tasks. They

can translate text from one language to another with impressive accuracy and fluency. This capability has significant implications for businesses operating in multilingual environments and global markets.

By leveraging GPT models, businesses and organizations can automate processes, improve customer experiences, generate high-quality content, and gain valuable insights from textual data. These models have the potential to revolutionize various industries by enabling advanced language understanding and generation.

Throughout this book, we will explore these use cases in more detail, providing practical examples and showcasing the immense potential of GPT models in real-world scenarios. So, let's dive deeper into the realm of OpenAI's GPT models and uncover the exciting possibilities they offer.

Note: The examples provided in this chapter are intended to illustrate the capabilities of GPT models. The specific implementation details may vary depending on the framework or platform used for integration.

Chapter 6

Installation Open AI [23]

Section 6.1: To set up an OpenAI account, you can follow these steps:

1. **Visit the OpenAI website:** Go to the OpenAI website at https://www.openai.com/.

2. **Sign up for an account:** Click on the "Get started" or "Sign up" button on the OpenAI homepage. You will be directed to the account creation page.

3. **Provide your information:** Fill in the required information to create your OpenAI account. This typically includes your name, email address, and a secure password. Make sure to read and accept the terms of service and privacy policy.

4. **Verify your email:** OpenAI will send you a verification email to the email address you provided during the

---

[23] https://openai.com/.

signup process. Go to your email inbox, open the verification email, and click on the provided link to verify your email address.

5. **Set up two-factor authentication (optional):** OpenAI highly recommends enabling two-factor authentication (2FA) for added security. Follow the instructions provided by OpenAI to set up 2FA for your account.

6. **Create an API key:** Once you have verified your email and logged into your OpenAI account, you can generate an API key. An API key is required to access OpenAI's API services, including GPT-3.5. Navigate to the API section of your account settings and follow the instructions to generate an API key. Make sure to securely store your API key as it grants access to your OpenAI resources.

7. **Review the documentation:** Familiarize yourself with the OpenAI documentation, which provides detailed information on how to use the OpenAI API, including guidelines, examples, and API reference documentation. The documentation will help you understand how to integrate OpenAI services into your applications.

By following these steps, you can successfully set up an OpenAI account. Remember to keep your account information and API key secure. If you encounter any issues or have further questions, you can reach out to OpenAI support for assistance.

Section 6.2 OpenAI Product Offering [24]

Three types of product offering are available in

OpenAI offers a variety of products and services, including:

APIs: OpenAI offers a variety of APIs that allow developers to access its language models. These APIs can be used to generate text, translate languages, write different kinds of creative content, and answer your questions in an informative way.

Products: OpenAI also offers a number of products that are built on top of its language models. These products include DALL-E 2, which can generate images from text descriptions, and CLIP, which can identify and match images to text descriptions.

Research: OpenAI is also a research organization that is working on developing new and improved language models. The results of this research are made available to the public through OpenAI's blog and research papers.

---

[24] https://openai.com/.

Here are some of OpenAI's most popular products and services:

ChatGPT is a language model developed by OpenAI. ChatGPT is trained on a large dataset containing vast amounts of text data from the internet, allowing it to learn patterns, context, and language usage.[25]

GPT-3: GPT-3 is a large language model that can generate text, translate languages, write different kinds of creative content, and answer your questions in an informative way.

GPT-4: Most advanced version of GPT-3 and it trained with more parameter as compare to GPT3

DALL-E 2: DALL-E 2 is a large language model that can generate images from text descriptions.[26]

CLIP: CLIP is a large language model that can identify and match images to text descriptions[27].

Whisper: Whisper is a web-based automatic speech recognition (ASR) system that can transcribe speech into text.[28]

---

[25] https://openai.com/chatgpt
[26] https://openai.com/dall-e-2
[27] https://openai.com/research/clip
[28] https://openai.com/search?q=WHISPER

Forefront: Forefront is a security framework that can be used to protect OpenAI's language models from misuse

Section 6.2: What is ChatGPT

ChatGPT:

It is available as a product offering in the OpenAI

ChatGPT is a language model developed by OpenAI. It is based on the GPT (Generative Pre-trained Transformer) architecture, specifically designed for generating human-like text in a conversational manner. ChatGPT is trained on a large dataset containing vast amounts of text data from the internet, allowing it to learn patterns, context, and language usage.

The purpose of ChatGPT is to provide a conversational agent that can engage in dialogue and respond to user inputs in a coherent and contextually appropriate manner. It can be used for a wide range of applications such as chatbots, virtual assistants, customer support systems, and more.

ChatGPT takes a user's input text and generates a response based on the context of the conversation. It is capable of understanding and generating text across various topics and can provide informative, creative, and contextually relevant responses. ChatGPT has the ability to handle prompts and follow-up questions, making it suitable for interactive and dynamic conversations.

It's important to note that while ChatGPT is a powerful language model, it is still an AI system and has limitations. It may occasionally produce incorrect or nonsensical responses and can be sensitive to input phrasing. OpenAI continuously works on improving the system's capabilities and addressing its limitations through ongoing research and development.

Overall, ChatGPT is a language model designed to facilitate natural and engaging conversations with users, enabling a wide range of conversational AI applications.

Section 6.3: Azure equivalent of Chat GPT

Azure does not have an exact equivalent to OpenAI's ChatGPT available as a pre-built service. Azure Cognitive Services provides various AI services, including natural language understanding, but it does not have a specific service that directly corresponds to the conversational capabilities of ChatGPT.

However, Azure provides a range of services that can be used to build and deploy conversational AI solutions. For example, you can use Azure Bot Service to create and deploy chatbots that can understand and respond to user queries. Additionally,

Azure offers language understanding capabilities through services like Language Understanding (LUIS) and Azure Cognitive Search, which can be combined to build more sophisticated conversational experiences.

To create a ChatGPT-like conversational AI solution in Azure, you would typically use a combination of these services along with custom application development. This involves designing conversation flows, training language models, implementing natural language processing, and integrating with Azure's AI services and tools.

It's worth mentioning that Azure Cognitive Services and Azure Machine Learning also provide powerful capabilities for natural language processing and text analysis, which can be used to enhance the language understanding and response generation components of your conversational AI solution.

While Azure does not have a pre-built service that directly matches ChatGPT, it offers a comprehensive set of tools and services that can be used to build sophisticated conversational AI applications tailored to your specific needs.

Section 6.4: Compare ChatGPT with Azure OpenAI Offering

ChatGPT and Azure OpenAI are both offerings from OpenAI, but they differ in terms of their specific features and implementation.

ChatGPT:

1. **Language Model:** ChatGPT is a specific variant of the GPT (Generative Pre-trained Transformer) language model designed for conversational interactions.

2. **Text Generation:** ChatGPT focuses on generating human-like text responses in a conversational manner.

3. **OpenAI API:** ChatGPT is accessible through the OpenAI API, which allows developers to integrate it into their applications and services.

4. **Fine-Tuning:** ChatGPT supports fine-tuning, enabling users to customize and adapt the model's behavior for specific use cases.

5. **OpenAI Playground:** ChatGPT has an interactive web interface called the OpenAI Playground, where users can test and experiment with the model.

Azure OpenAI:

1. **Azure Integration:** Azure OpenAI is a specific integration of OpenAI services within the Microsoft Azure cloud platform.

2. **Diverse OpenAI Models:** Azure OpenAI provides access to various OpenAI models, including ChatGPT, but also other models like GPT-3 and Codex.

3. **Deployment and Management:** Azure OpenAI offers tools and resources for deploying, scaling, and managing OpenAI models within the Azure environment.

4. **Azure CLI and SDKs:** Azure OpenAI provides command-line interfaces (CLI) and software development kits (SDKs) for developers to interact with OpenAI services within Azure.

5. **Azure Ecosystem:** Azure OpenAI is part of the larger Azure ecosystem, which includes a wide range of cloud services and integrations, enabling seamless integration with other Azure offerings.

In summary, ChatGPT is a specific variant of the GPT language model developed by OpenAI, focusing on generating conversational text responses. Azure OpenAI, on the other hand, is a suite of OpenAI services integrated within the Microsoft Azure cloud platform, providing access to various OpenAI models, including ChatGPT, along with additional tools and resources for deployment and management within the Azure environment.

Feature	ChatGPT	Azure OpenAI
Language Model	Variant of GPT	Various OpenAI models (including ChatGPT)
Text Generation	Conversational text responses	Text generation and other AI capabilities
OpenAI API	Accessible through OpenAI API	Integrated within Microsoft Azure
Fine-Tuning	Supports fine-tuning for customization	Flexible deployment and management
OpenAI Playground	Interactive web interface for testing	Command-line interfaces (CLI) and SDKs
Azure Integration	Not directly integrated with Azure	Integrated within the Azure cloud platform
Deployment	N/A	Tools and resources for deployment and scaling
Azure CLI/SDKs	N/A	CLI and SDKs for Azure ecosystem integration
Ecosystem	Standalone OpenAI offering	Part of the broader Azure cloud service ecosystem

Section 6.5: What is DALL-E 2

DALL-E 2, an expansive language model (LLM) engineered by OpenAI, possesses the remarkable ability to craft images based on textual descriptions. Through training on an extensive collection of text-image pairs, this model can produce realistic images spanning a diverse spectrum of objects and scenarios.

For instance, by providing DALL-E 2 with a textual prompt like "a photorealistic painting of a cat riding a unicorn on a rainbow," it can generate an image that precisely corresponds to the given description. Moreover, DALL-E 2 has the capability to generate images of objects that exist only within the realm of imagination, such as "a flying board" or "a talking cow."

Though DALL-E 2 is currently undergoing refinement, it has already demonstrated its proficiency in generating captivating images. The potential applications for this model are wide-ranging, encompassing tasks like crafting marketing visuals, conceptualizing product designs, and generating artistic compositions.

Key Features of DALL-E 2:

Image Synthesis: DALL-E 2 excels in producing images based on textual input, bridging the gap between language and visuals.

Versatility: The model can generate images of both real-world and fictional subjects, catering to a diverse range of creative scenarios.

Innovative Applications: DALL-E 2's potential extends to diverse fields, including marketing, product design, and artistic creation.

Can edit existing images: DALL-E 2 can edit existing images by adding or removing objects, changing the colors, or adjusting the lighting.

Can create variations of an image: DALL-E 2 can create variations of an image by changing the pose, expression, or background.

Note this is also available in Azure OpenAI

As DALL-E 2 continues its development, its burgeoning capabilities hold promise for revolutionizing the way we create and interact with visual content.

DALL-E 2 Examples:

DALL-E 2, developed by OpenAI, is an advanced image generation model. It has various use cases across different industries. Here is an example use case of DALL-E 2:

Creative Content Generation: DALL-E 2 can be used to create unique and realistic images for a wide range of creative purposes. For example, it can generate custom illustrations, artwork, and visual designs. This can be valuable for graphic designers, artists, marketers, and advertisers who need high-quality visuals to enhance their projects.

Additionally, DALL-E 2 can assist in creating product mock-ups, generating images for social media posts, and visualizing concepts for presentations. Its ability to generate novel and imaginative images opens up endless possibilities for creative content creation.

By leveraging DALL-E 2, businesses and individuals can save time and resources by automating the image generation process. It eliminates the need for extensive manual design work and provides access to a vast library of generated images that can be customized to specific requirements.

Overall, DALL-E 2 empowers users to bring their creative visions to life by generating visually stunning and unique images, enabling a new level of creativity and efficiency in various industries.

Section 6.6: APIs as Product in OpenAI

OpenAI provides several APIs that developers can use to access their language models and other services. Some examples of OpenAI APIs are:

1. GPT-3 API: This API allows developers to integrate the GPT-3 language model into their applications. It enables tasks such as text generation, translation, summarization, and question-answering.

2. DALL-E API: This API provides access to the DALL-E model, which generates unique and creative images from textual descriptions. Developers can use this API to create custom images based on specific input.

3. Codex API: OpenAI's Codex API allows developers to convert natural language into executable code. It is designed to assist with code generation, code completion, and other programming-related tasks.

4. Whisper API: The Whisper API is used for automatic speech recognition (ASR). It converts spoken language into written text, making it useful for applications involving transcription, voice assistants, and more.

These are just a few examples of the APIs offered by OpenAI. Each API serves a specific purpose and provides developers with access to different functionalities of OpenAI's models.

Section 6.7 Steps to call OpenAI:

To call an OpenAI model in your program using an API, you can follow these steps:

1. Obtain API credentials: Sign up for an account with OpenAI and obtain the necessary API credentials, such as an API key or access token. This will allow you to authenticate and access the OpenAI API.

2. Choose an API client: Select a programming language or framework that you want to use to interact with the OpenAI API. OpenAI provides official API clients for popular languages like Python, which can simplify the integration process.

3. Install the API client: Install the OpenAI API client library for your chosen programming language. This library will provide convenient methods and functions for making API calls and handling responses.

4. Import the API client: Import the necessary modules or libraries from the API client into your program.

5. Authenticate with the API: Use your API credentials to authenticate your program with the OpenAI API. This typically involves passing your API key or access token to the client library.

6. Construct your API request: Determine the specific API endpoint and parameters you need to use for your desired task. For example, if you want to generate text, you would use the "completions" endpoint and specify the input prompt.

7. Make the API call: Use the appropriate method or function from the API client library to make the API call. Pass in the necessary parameters and data required for your request.

8. Receive and process the API response: Capture the response from the API call and process the data returned by the OpenAI model. This may involve parsing the JSON response, extracting relevant information, and incorporating it into your program's logic.

9. Handle errors and exceptions: Implement error handling and exception handling mechanisms to gracefully handle any issues that may occur during the

API call or response processing. This ensures your program can recover or provide appropriate feedback to the user.

10. Integrate the API response into your program: Utilize the output or data from the OpenAI model's API response within your program as needed. This could involve displaying generated text, incorporating the results into further processing steps, or any other relevant actions.

Example Steps for of calling an OpenAI model using Python and the OpenAI API

In this example, we use the OpenAI Python library to interact with the OpenAI API.

1. Install the OpenAI package: Use pip or condo to install the OpenAI Python package by running the following command:

Copy code

pip install OpenAI

2.Set up OpenAI credentials: Obtain your OpenAI API key from the OpenAI website. Once you have your API key, you need to set it as an environment variable in your Python script. You can do this by using the following code snippet:

import os

3.Add Authentication key:to authenticate the API

os.environ["OPENAI_API_KEY"] = "YOUR_API_KEY

4. Next, we define a prompt as the starting point for generating text. You can customize the promptbased on your specific use case.

5. Then, we make a call to the openai.Completion.create() method, specifying the engine (e.g., 'davinci') and the prompt. You can also set additional parameters like max_tokens to control the length of the generated text.

6. The API response is stored in the response variable, and we extract the generated text from response.choices[0].text. We remove any leading or trailing whitespace using strip().

7. Finally, we print the generated text to see the output of the OpenAI model.

```python
#Text Generation using OpenAI

import openai

# Set up your API credentials
openai.api_key = 'YOUR_API_KEY'

# Define your prompt
prompt = 'Once upon a time'

# Generate text using the OpenAI API
response = openai.Completion.create(
  engine='davinc-model',
  prompt=prompt,
  max_tokens=100
)

# Access the generated text from the API response
generated_text = response.choices[0].text.strip()

# Print the generated text
print(generated_text)
```

SUMMARY & CONCLUSION

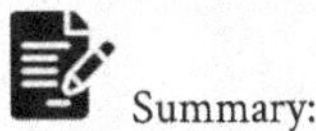 Summary:

OpenAI is a research and development company focused on developing safe and beneficial artificial general intelligence (AGI). They offer a range of products and APIs built on top of their large language models. Some notable products include DALL-E 2, GPT-3, Whisper, and Forefront. OpenAI publishes research papers and blog posts covering various AI topics and is dedicated to creating educational resources about AI and its societal impact.

 Conclusion:

OpenAI is a leading company in AGI research and development. Their products, such as DALL-E 2, GPT-3, Whisper, and Forefront, have the potential to bring significant benefits to industries and fields. DALL-E 2 enables the creation of realistic and creative images, GPT-3 offers text generation, translation, and informative responses, Whisper provides speech-to-text transcription, and Forefront safeguards against misuse of language models. OpenAI's commitment to safe and beneficial AGI sets them on a path to make a positive impact across various sectors.

Note All the models in the OpenAI are available in Azure OpenAI and Azure Cloud infrastructure are enterprise grade compliance are available in the Azure OpenAI.

CHAPTER 6 QUIZ: TEST YOUR SKILLS

1. Which of the following is a large language model developed by OpenAI?

   - ChatGPT

   - DALL-E

   - GPT-3

   - Whisper

2. Which of the following can generate images from text6descriptions?

   - ChatGPT

   - DALL-E

   - GPT-3

   - Whisper

3. Which of the following is a web-based automatic speech recognition system?

   - ChatGPT

   - DALL-E

- GPT-3

- Whisper

4. Which of the following is a security framework that can be used to protect OpenAI's language models from misuse?

    - ChatGPT

    - DALL-E

    - GPT-3

    - Forefront

5. Which of the following is still under development but has the potential to be used for a variety of purposes, such as creating marketing materials, designing products, or generating art?

    - ChatGPT

    - DALL-E

    - GPT-3

    - Whisper

6. Which of the following can generate photorealistic images of a wide variety of objects and scenes?

    - ChatGPT

- DALL-E

- GPT-3

- Whisper

7. Which of the following can generate images of objects that do not exist in the real world?

    - ChatGPT

    - DALL-E

    - GPT-3

    - Whisper

8. Which of the following can edit existing images by adding or removing objects, changing the colors, or adjusting the lighting?

    - ChatGPT

    - DALL-E

    - GPT-3

    - Whisper

CHAPTER 6 QUIZ: ANSWERS

1. Which of the following is a large language model developed by OpenAI?

   Answer: GPT-3

2. Which of the following can generate images from text descriptions?

   Answer: DALL-E

3. Which of the following is a web-based automatic speech recognition system?

   Answer: Whisper

4. Which of the following is a security framework that can be used to protect OpenAI's language models from misuse?

   Answer: Forefront

5. Which of the following is still under development but has the potential to be used for a variety of purposes, such as creating marketing materials, designing products, or generating art?

   Answer: DALL-E

6. Which of the following can generate photorealistic images of a wide variety of objects and scenes?

Answer: DALL-E

7. Which of the following can generate images of objects that do not exist in the real world?

   Answer: DALL-E

8. Which of the following can edit existing images by adding or removing objects, changing the colors, or adjusting the lighting?

   Answer: DALL-E

Chapter 7

Installation Azure Open AI

Section 7.1: Install and set up the Azure CLI for OpenAI

To install and set up the Azure CLI for OpenAI, you can follow these steps:

1.**Check the system requirements:** Ensure that your system meets the requirements for installing and running the Azure CLI. You can find the system requirements in the Azure CLI documentation[29].

2.**Install the Azure CLI:** Visit the official Azure CLI installation guide for your operating system (Windows, macOS, or Linux) and follow the instructions provided. The installation guide provides different installation methods, such as using package managers, direct downloads, or running scripts[30].

---

[29] Azure CLI documentation: https://docs.microsoft.com/en-us/cli/azure/

[30] Install Azure CLI on Windows: https://docs.microsoft.com/en-us/cli/azure/install-azure-cli-windows

3.Verify the installation: Open a command prompt or terminal window and run the following command to verify that the Azure CLI has been installed successfully:

```
```

```
az --version
```

```
```

4.Sign in to Azure: Run the following command and follow the prompts to sign in to your Azure account:

```
```

```
az login
```

```
```

5.Set the default subscription: If you have multiple Azure subscriptions, you can set the default subscription for the CLI using the following command:

```
```

```
az account set --subscription <subscription_id>
```

```
```

6.Install the OpenAI extension: The OpenAI CLI extension provides additional commands and functionality specific to

---

Install Azure CLI on macOS: https://docs.microsoft.com/en-us/cli/azure/install-azure-cli-macos

Install Azure CLI on Linux: https://docs.microsoft.com/en-us/cli/azure/install-azure-cli-linux

OpenAI services. Run the following command to install the OpenAI extension:

```
az extension add --name openai
```

7.Configure the OpenAI API credentials: To authenticate with the OpenAI API, you need to set the OpenAI API key. You can do this by running the following command:

```
az configure --defaults openai-davinci-codex=<your_openai_api_key>
```

Replace `<your_openai_api_key>` with your actual OpenAI API key. This step configures the default API key for the OpenAI Davinci Codex model.

With Environment Variables : In order to use the Azure OpenAI module, you need to set up your environment variables. These variables will store your Azure OpenAI resource ID, resource key, and deployment name. You can find these values in the Azure OpenAI Studio.

export OPENAI_RESOURCE_ID=<your-resource-id>

export OPENAI_RESOURCE_KEY=<your-resource-key>

export OPENAI_DEPLOYMENT_NAME=<your-deployment-name>

8.Verify the OpenAI extension installation: Run the following command to verify that the OpenAI extension has been installed successfully:

```
```az openai --help```
```

This command will display the available commands and options provided by the OpenAI CLI extension.

Test your installation. Once you have completed all of the previous steps, you can test your installation by running the following command:

```
az openai completions --prompt "What is Wikipedia?"
```
```

Section 7.2: Steps to create an Azure account: Access OpenAI services & Install Azure OpenAI using Azure portal

To use OpenAI services on Azure, you can follow these steps to set up and configure OpenAI using the Azure portal:

1. **1.Sign in to the Azure portal:** Go to the Azure portal website (https://portal.azure.com) and sign in with your Azure account credentials.

2. **Create a new resource:** Click on the "Create a resource" button in the Azure portal.

3. **Search for OpenAI:** In the search bar, type "OpenAI" and press Enter. From the search results, select the desired OpenAI service you want to use, such as "OpenAI GPT-3" or "OpenAI Chatbot."

4. **Configure the service:** Provide the required information and configuration settings for the OpenAI service. This may include specifying the subscription, resource group, region, pricing tier, and other options based on the specific service you selected.

5. **Review and create:** Double-check the provided configurations, and then click on the "Review + Create" button.

6. **Create the resource:** After reviewing the configurations, click on the "Create" button to create the OpenAI resource.

7. **Wait for deployment:** The Azure portal will initiate the deployment process, which may take a few minutes. You can monitor the deployment progress in the portal.

8. **Access and use the OpenAI service:** Once the deployment is complete, you can access and use the OpenAI service as per the documentation and instructions provided by Azure and OpenAI. This may involve using APIs, SDKs, or specific tools depending on the service you selected.

Section7.3 Installation Screen Shots Step-By-Step:

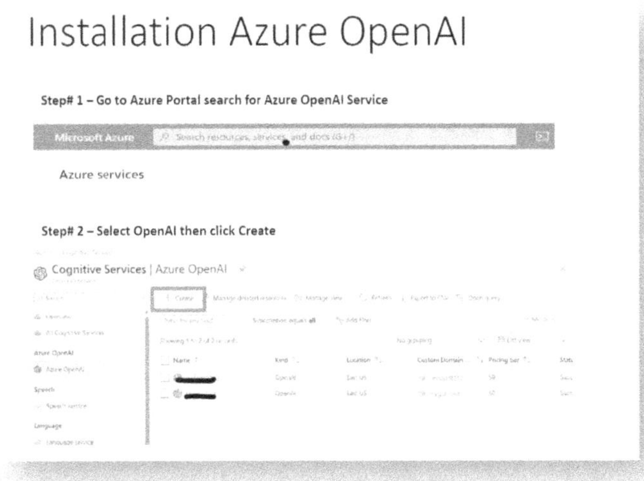

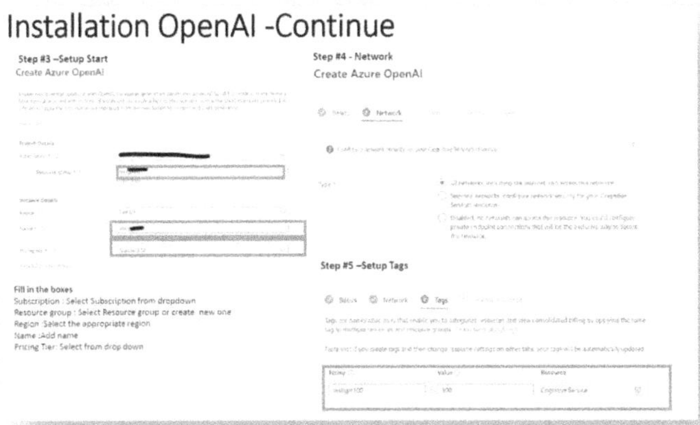

Installation OpenAI -Continue

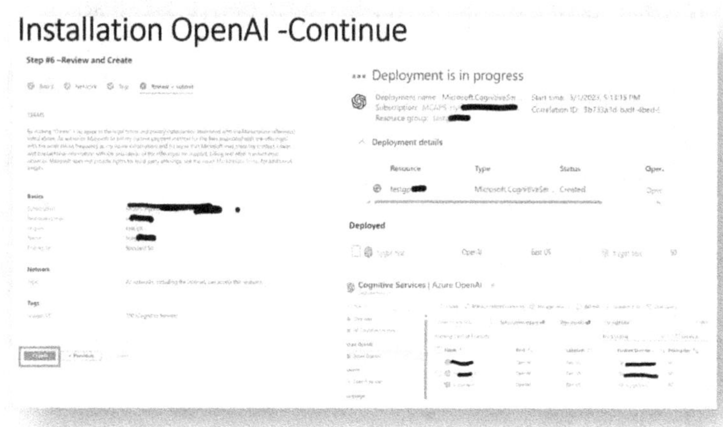

Section 7.4 : Understanding the Portal -Azure OpenAI

After Deployment

Step #7

After deployment go back to the Azure Portal and select the resource deployed

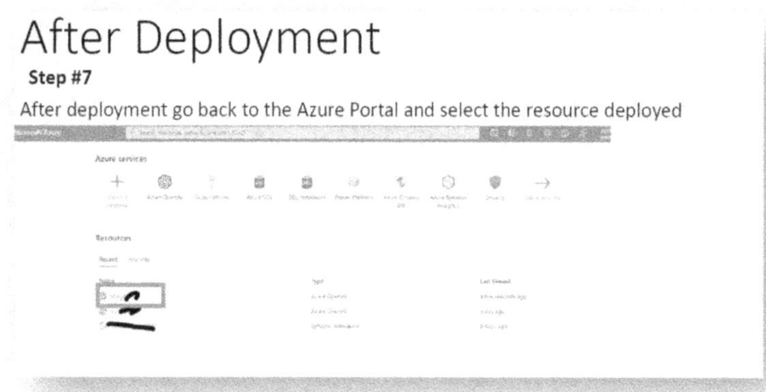

After Deployment-Continue

Step #7

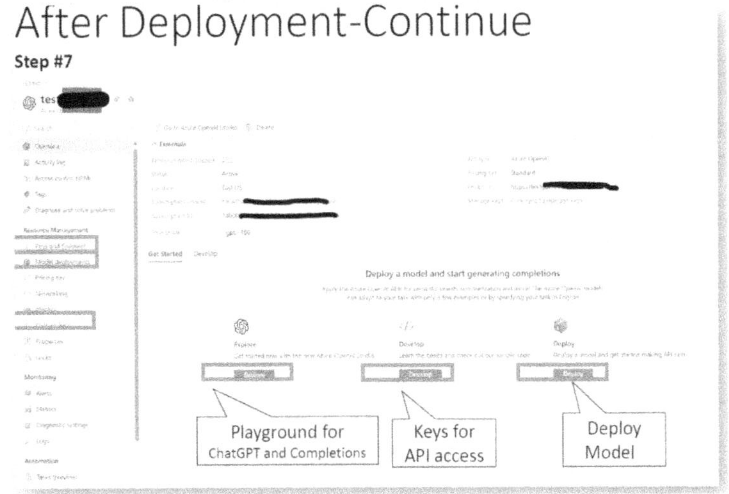

Explore: Give access to the Azure OpenAI studio. It provides the playground, the OpenAI Playground is an interactive online platform that allows users to experiment and interact with OpenAI's language models.

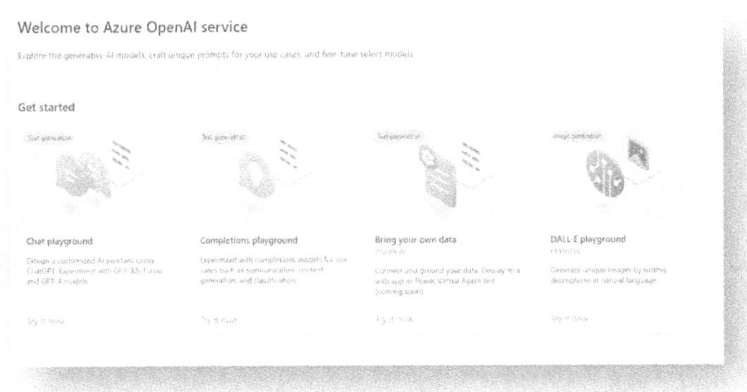

Develop (Keys and Endpoints): API keys are available and also have information about how to recycle keys and copy the keys.

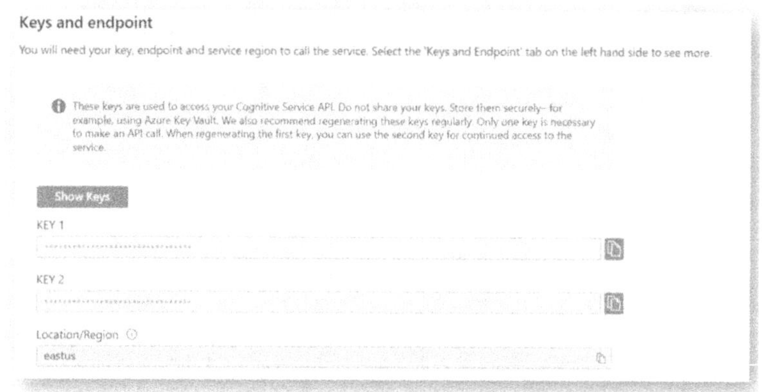

Deploy: Give the details about how to deploy the model and edit the deployment model

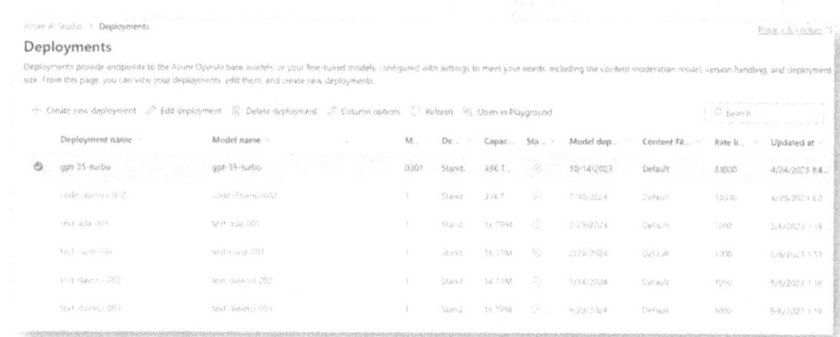

Section 7.5: After Deployment – How to Deploy Models [31]

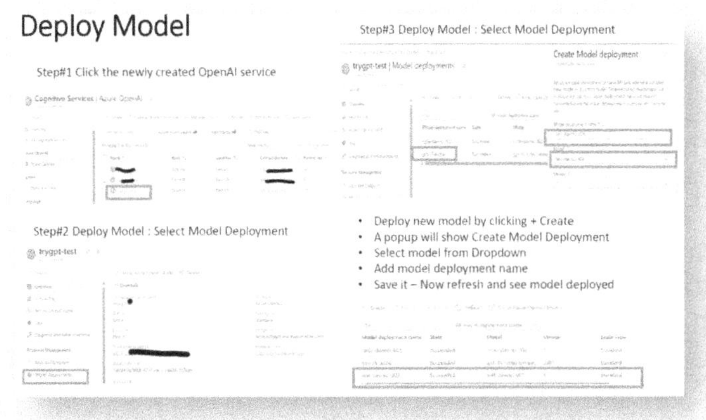

Section 7.6: Steps for Deploying a Model:

1.Go to Azure Open Studio: Select the Model Deployment

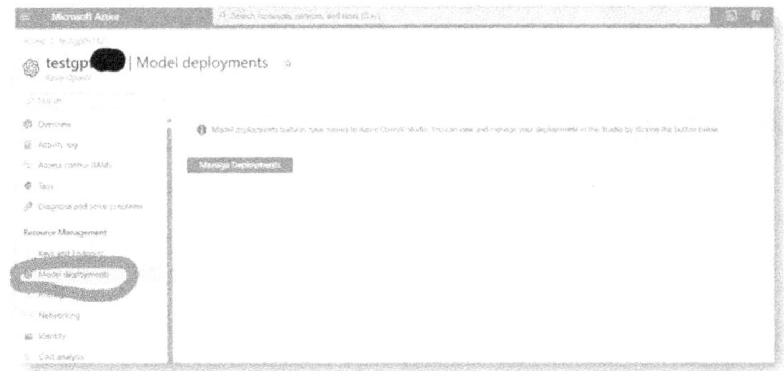

---

[31] https://docs.microsoft.com/azure/openai/

2.Click Manage Deployments

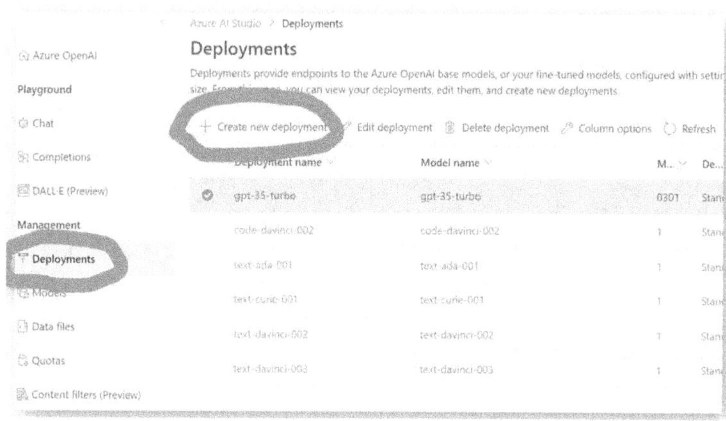

3.Click "+ Create New Deployment."

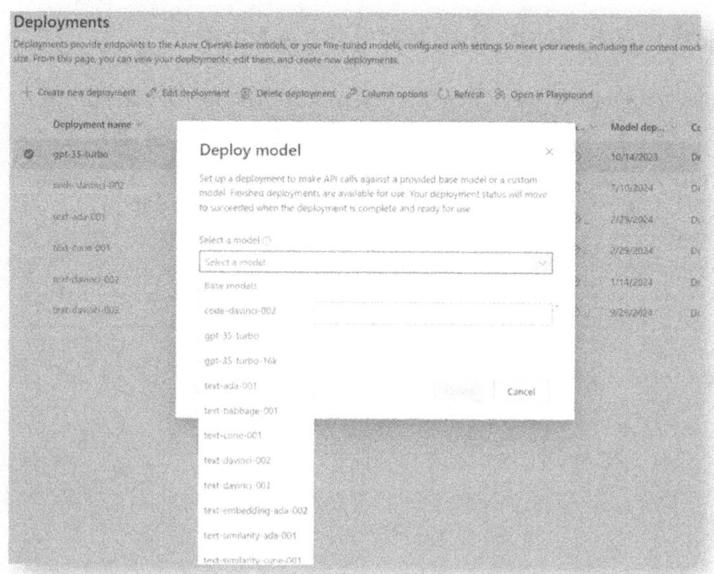

4.Select a model – *"Select the Model need to deployment "*

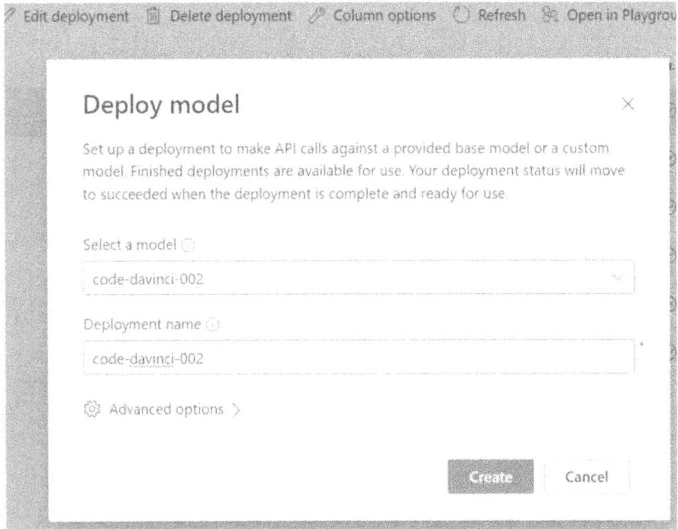

5.Click the Advance options

Select the Token Per Limit

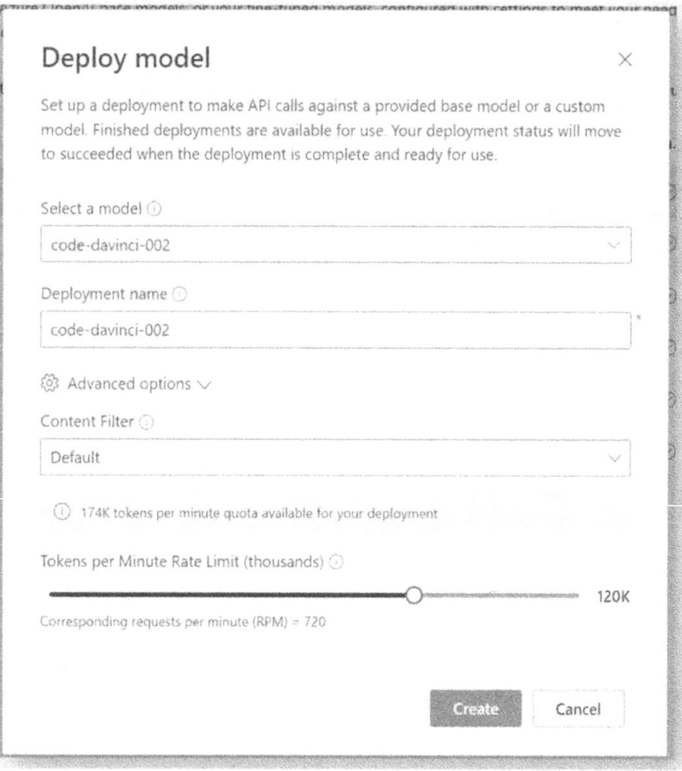
Deploy model
Set up a deployment to make API calls against a provided base model or a custom model. Finished deployments are available for use. Your deployment status will move to succeeded when the deployment is complete and ready for use.
Select a model
code-davinci-002
Deployment name
code-davinci-002
Advanced options
Content Filter
Default
174K tokens per minute quota available for your deployment
Tokens per Minute Rate Limit (thousands)
120K
Corresponding requests per minute (RPM) = 720
Create
Cancel

Section 7.6: Understanding Azure OpenAI playground, Azure OpenAI Services and APIs etc.

Select the Explore section in the Azure Studio

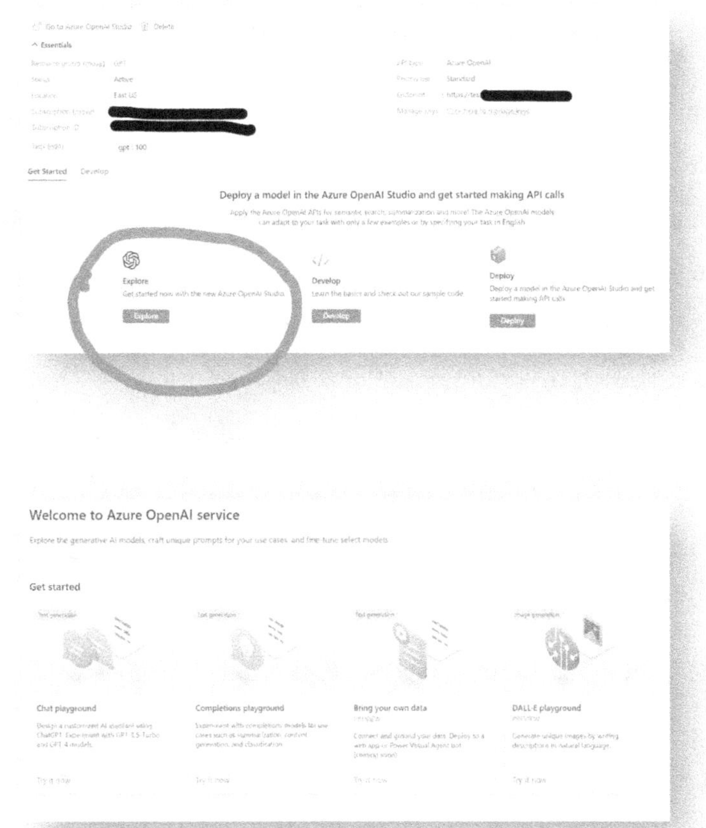

This gives the four Services as shown in the figure:

Chat Playground

Completion Playground

Bring your own data

DALL-E Playground

Let's discuss more about the Playground: (**Note: This function also implies to OpenAI & Azur OpenAI**)

The OpenAI Playground is an interactive online platform that allows users to experiment and interact with OpenAI's language models. It provides a user-friendly interface where you can input text prompts and see the model generate responses in real-time. The Playground is a great way to learn about how GPT-3 works and to experiment with its capabilities. You can use it to generate different creative text formats, like poems, code, scripts, musical pieces, email, letters, etc., and to answer your questions in an informative way, even if they are open ended, challenging, or strange.

The Playground offers access to various OpenAI models, including GPT-3 and GPT-4 (in preview), allowing users to explore the capabilities of these models. It is designed to showcase the power and versatility of OpenAI's language models and provide a hands-on experience for users to experiment with text generation. The Playground is also a great way to get started with OpenAI's API. If you want to use GPT-

3 in your own applications, you can use the Playground to learn about the API and to test out your code.

The Playground is divided into two main sections: the "Prompt" section and the "Response" section. Users can enter prompts or instructions in the text input area, and the model will generate a response based on the input. The Playground also provides options to customize the behavior of the model, such as adjusting the temperature to control the randomness of the output.

Additionally, the Playground offers features like code completions, allowing users to explore how the models can assist in programming tasks. It supports various programming languages and can generate code snippets based on the provided context.

The OpenAI Playground is a valuable tool for developers, researchers, and curious individuals who want to explore and understand the capabilities of OpenAI's language models. It provides an accessible and interactive environment to interact with the models and generate text outputs based on given prompts or code snippets.

Section 7.6.1 Chat Playground: (Note: This function also implies to OpenAI & Azur OpenAI)

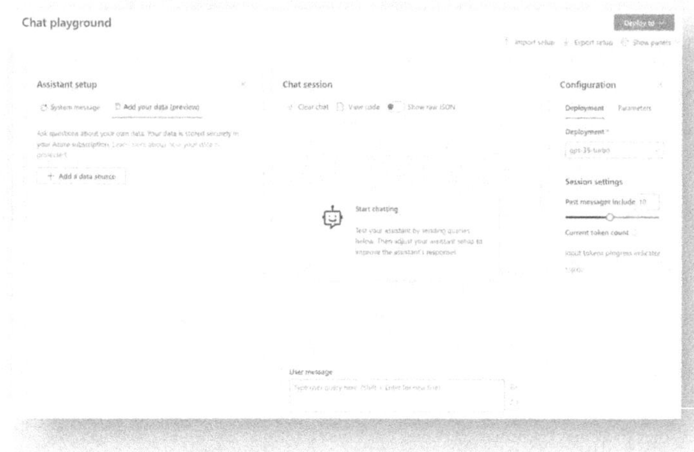

The Chat Playground is an interactive web-based tool provided by OpenAI that allows users to have dynamic conversations with language models like GPT-3. It offers a user-friendly interface where you can engage in back-and-forth exchanges with the model, simulating a conversation with an AI.

In the Chat Playground, you can enter a series of messages as input, alternating between user messages and model messages. You start the conversation with a user message, and the model responds accordingly. You can continue the conversation by adding more messages, and the model will generate appropriate responses based on the context and the provided input.

The Chat Playground provides a versatile platform to explore various use cases. You can ask questions, get information, seek advice, or have creative exchanges with the model. It allows you to experiment with different prompts and observe how the model interprets and generates responses based on the given conversation history.

The tool also offers options to customize the behavior of the model. You can provide system-level instructions to guide the model's behavior, such as specifying a persona or setting the tone of the conversation. Additionally, you can adjust parameters like temperature and max tokens to control the creativity and length of the model's responses.

The Chat Playground is designed to facilitate interactive and iterative conversations with language models. It provides a convenient way to test and refine your conversational prompts, explore the model's capabilities, and gain insights into its language generation abilities.

Please note that my knowledge is based on information available up until September 2021, and there may have been updates or changes to the Chat Playground since then. For the most up-to-date information and access to the Chat Playground, I recommend visiting the official OpenAI website or referring to the OpenAI documentation.

Section 7.6.2 Setup in Chat Playground:

Three Sections in a Playground:

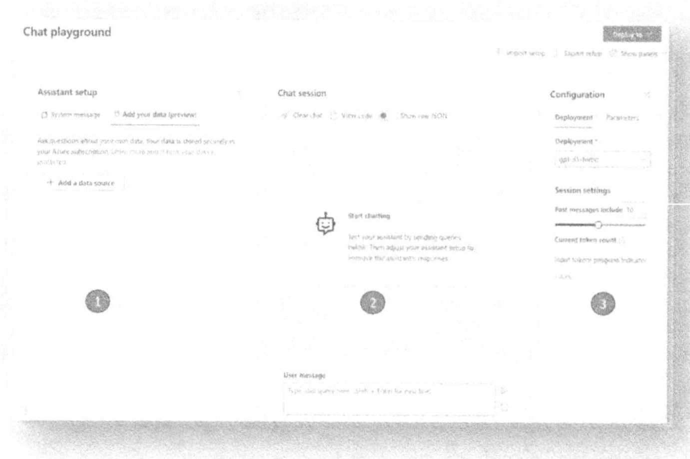

Section 1: Assistance Setup:

In the OpenAI Chat Playground, there are several components that contribute to its functionality and user experience. Let's describe each component:

1. **Chat Interface:** The chat interface is the main area where you can interact with the language model. It provides a conversation-like structure where you can input messages and receive model-generated

responses. You can enter your messages on the left side, and the model's responses will appear on the right side.

2. **User Messages:** User messages are the inputs provided by you. You can type your messages in the chat interface and press enter to send them to the model. User messages can be in the form of questions, prompts, or instructions to guide the model's behavior.

3. **Model Responses:** Model responses are the generated outputs from the language model based on the user messages. They appear on the right side of the chat interface and provide the model's answers, suggestions, or completion of the conversation based on the preceding messages.

4. **System Messages:** System messages are special messages displayed in the chat interface that provide additional instructions or guidance to the model. They are displayed in a different style or color to differentiate them from user and model messages. System messages are used to set the context or behavior for the model.

5. **Configuration Options:** The chat playground may include configuration options that allow you to customize the behavior of the model. These options can vary depending on the specific implementation of the

playground and the capabilities of the underlying language model. Configuration options may include parameters like temperature, max tokens, and other settings that affect the output generated by the model.

1. **Temperature:** Temperature controls the randomness of the model's output. A higher temperature value (e.g., 0.8) will result in more random and creative responses, while a lower temperature (e.g., 0.2) will produce more focused and deterministic responses.

2. **Max Tokens:** Max Tokens limits the length of the response generated by the model. By setting a specific value, you can control the number of tokens (words or characters) in the output. This can be useful to ensure that the response is not too lengthy or to set a specific response length requirement.

3. **Other Parameters:** The Chat Playground may also provide additional parameters that can be adjusted to fine-tune the model's behavior. These parameters might include options to control the response style, verbosity, or other aspects of the generated output. The specific parameters available may vary depending on the version of the model and the configuration of the playground.

6. **Interactive Conversation:** The chat playground enables interactive conversations where you can have back-and-forth exchanges with the model. You can ask questions, provide prompts, or engage in a dialogue to explore the capabilities of the language model and receive responses in real-time.

7. **Evaluation and Experimentation:** The chat playground serves as a platform for evaluating and experimenting with different inputs and configurations. You can test the model's responses to various prompts, refine your instructions, and observe how the model generates text based on different inputs.

Overall, the chat playground combines the input and output capabilities of a language model in a conversational format, providing an interactive environment to explore and interact with the model's responses.

Section 7.6.3 Configuration:

Parameters:

Parameters in Azure OpenAI Chat Playground:

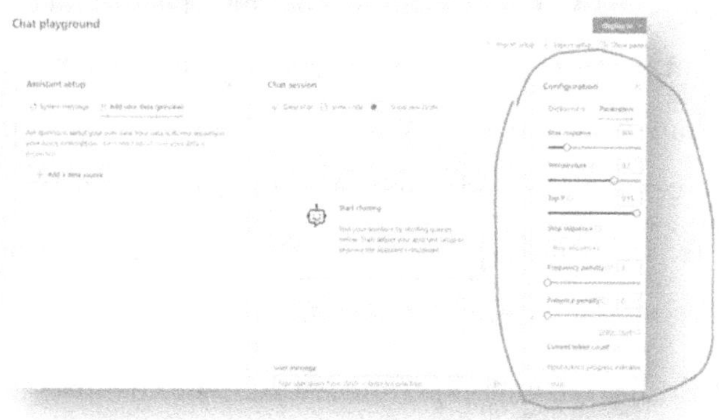

1. **Max Response Length:** Sets the maximum length of the generated response in terms of characters. You can specify the maximum number of characters you want the response to be limited to.

2. **Temperature:** Controls the randomness of the model's responses. A higher temperature value (e.g., 0.8) produces more diverse and creative outputs, while a lower value (e.g., 0.2) generates more focused and deterministic responses.

3. **Top P:** Specifies the cumulative probability threshold for the model's output tokens. It limits the set of tokens the model considers when generating a response, based on their cumulative probabilities. A higher value (e.g., 0.8) allows for more diversity and exploration, while a

lower value (e.g., 0.2) prioritizes more likely and safer completions.

4. **Stop Sequence:** Defines a sequence of tokens that, when encountered in the model's response, indicates the end of the generated output. It can be a specific word, phrase, or combination of tokens that you want to act as a stopping point for the model.

5. **Frequency Penalty:** Discourages the model from repeating the same or similar responses. A higher penalty value (e.g., 1.2) makes the model less likely to generate repetitive answers, while a lower value (e.g., 0.8) allows for more frequent repetition.

6. **Presence Penalty:** Encourages or discourages the usage of specific tokens in the model's response. A higher penalty value (e.g., 1.2) discourages the model from using tokens it has already used, promoting more diverse outputs, while a lower value (e.g., 0.8) allows for repeated usage of tokens.

These parameters give you control over aspects such as response length, randomness, diversity, stopping points, repetition, and token usage, allowing you to customize the behavior and output of the model to better suit your needs.

Section 7.6.4 Deployment:

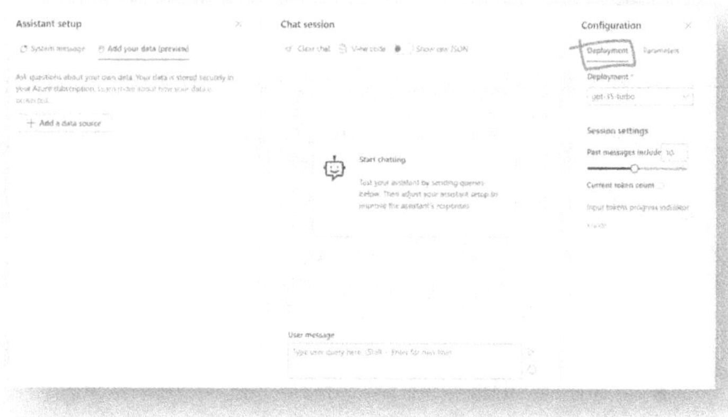

Here are the summarized descriptions of the deployment-related parameters and indicators in Azure OpenAI Chat Playground:

1. Deployment: This parameter allows you to select the specific deployment of the OpenAI model you want to use. It refers to the specific version or instance of the model that is deployed and accessible for generating responses.

2. Session Settings: These settings define the configuration for the current chat session. It includes parameters such as the model, temperature, max tokens, top p, stop sequence, frequency penalty, and presence penalty. You can adjust these settings to control the behavior and output of the model during the session.

3. Past Messages Included: This setting determines whether the past messages in the chat history should be included as part of the input when generating a response. By including past messages, you provide context to the model, allowing it to generate responses that take into account the conversation history.

4. Current Token Count: This indicator displays the current number of tokens used in the input message. It helps you keep track of the token usage and stay within the model's token limit.

5. Input Tokens Progress Indicator: This indicator shows the progress of the token count as you type the input message. It helps you monitor the token usage in real-time and ensures that you do not exceed the token limit.

These deployment-related parameters and indicators in the Chat Playground provide control over the model's behavior, input history, and token usage, allowing you to manage the conversation and track the progress of your interaction with the OpenAI model.

Section 7.6.5 Completion Playground: (Note: This function also implies to OpenAI & Azur OpenAI)

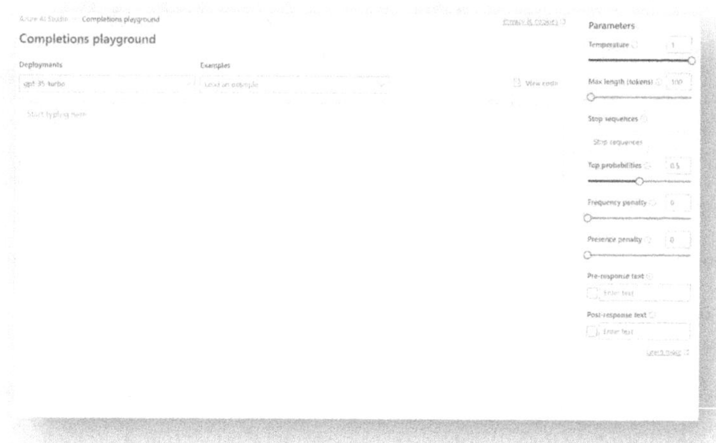

The Completion Playground is an interactive web-based tool provided by OpenAI that allows users to experiment and explore the capabilities of language models like GPT-3. It provides a user-friendly interface where you can input a prompt or an incomplete sentence and observe how the model completes it based on the context and the provided input.

The Completion Playground allows you to interact with the language model in real-time, providing you with immediate responses to your prompts. It can be used to generate text, answer questions, create stories, and much more. It gives you a hands-on experience of the model's capabilities and helps you understand how it responds to different inputs.

The tool also allows you to adjust parameters like temperature and max tokens to control the randomness and length of the generated completion. It provides options to refine and iterate on your prompts, enabling you to experiment and fine-tune the generated output according to your desired outcome.

The Completion Playground is a valuable resource for developers, researchers, and anyone interested in exploring the capabilities of language models. It offers an intuitive interface to interact with the models and gain insights into their behavior and performance.

Section 7.6.6 Bring your own data:

This is part of the Chat playground:

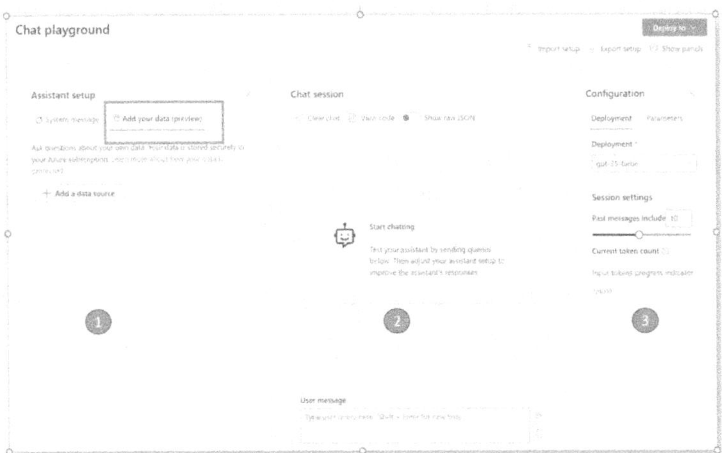

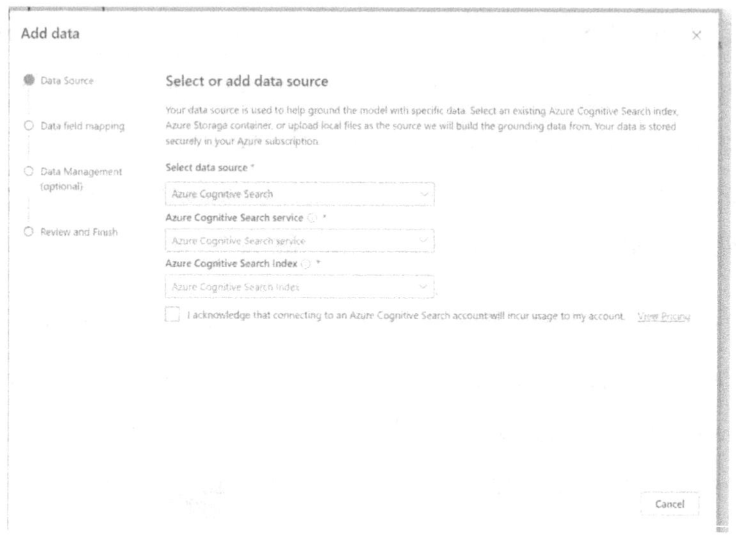

Bring Your Own Data (BYOD) feature is available in OpenAI. This allows you to train OpenAI's large language models (LLMs) on your own data. This can be useful if you have a specific domain of knowledge that you want the LLM to be aware of.

To use BYOD, you will need to create an Azure OpenAI resource in the Azure portal. Once you have created the resource, you can upload your data to an Azure Storage container. You can then use the Azure OpenAI Studio to train the LLM on your data.

The Azure OpenAI Studio is a web-based tool that makes it easy to train and deploy OpenAI's LLMs. In the studio, you can create a new project and select the BYOD option. You will then need to specify the location of your data and the LLM that you want to train.

To use BYOD with Azure OpenAI, you will need to create a storage account and a search index in Azure. You can then upload your data to the storage account and index it using the search index. Once your data is indexed, you can use it to train and fine-tune the OpenAI models[32].

Here are some of the benefits of using BYOD with Azure OpenAI:

Improved performance: BYOD can improve the performance of the OpenAI models by allowing you to train them on your own data. This can make the models more accurate for your specific needs.

Increased flexibility: BYOD gives you more flexibility in how you use the OpenAI models. You can use your own data to train the models and fine-tune them to your specific needs.

Increased security: BYOD can help you to improve the security of your data by allowing you to store it in your own storage

---

[32] https://azure.microsoft.com/en-us/updates/azure-open-ai-service-on-your-data/

account. You can also control who has access to your data and how it is used.

Here are the steps on how to bring your own data in Azure OpenAI in Azure Chat Playground:

1. Go to the Azure OpenAI Studio:
    https://oai.azure.com/.

2. Sign in with the credentials that have access to your Azure OpenAI resource.

3. Select the Chat playground tile.

4. On the Assistant setup tile, select Add your data (preview) > + Add a data source.

5. In the pane that appears, select Upload files under Select data source.

6. Azure OpenAI needs both a storage resource and a search resource to access and index your data. If you don't have these resources already, you can create them in the Azure Portal.

7. In the Upload files pane, select Browse for file and select the files you want to upload. Then select Upload files.

8. Select Next.

9. Review the details you entered, and select Save and close.

10. You can now chat with the model and it will use information from your data to construct the response.[33]

Section 7.6.7 DALL-E Playground

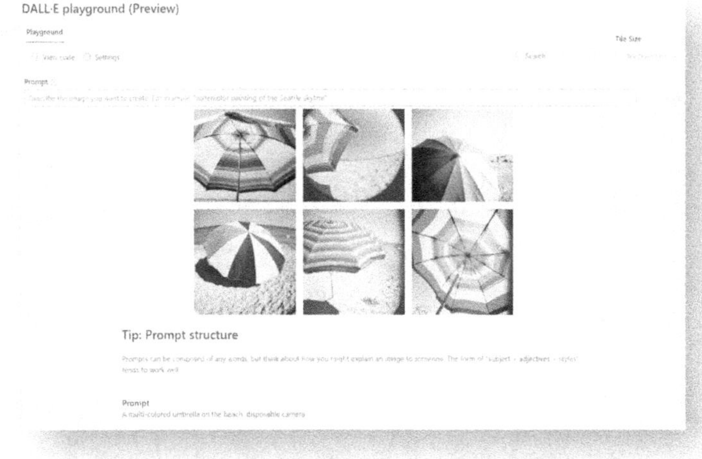

---

33 https://azure.microsoft.com/en-us/updates/azure-open-ai-service-on-your-data/

DALL-E Playground is a web-based tool that allows you to experiment with DALL-E, an artificial intelligence (AI) system that can create realistic images from text descriptions.

To use DALL-E Playground, you simply type a text description of the image you want to create into the prompt field. For example, you could type "a cat sitting on a skateboard" or "a painting of a city in the clouds." DALL-E will then generate an image based on your description.

You can also use the parameters section to adjust the settings for DALL-E. For example, you can specify the maximum size of the image, the number of images to generate, and the style of the images.

To generate an image, click on the "Generate" button. DALL-E will then generate an image based on your prompt and the settings that you have specified.

You can then use the "Edit" button to edit the image. You can also use the "Share" button to share the image with others.

DALL-E Playground is a great way to learn about how DALL-E works and to experiment with its capabilities. You can use it to create different creative images, like paintings, drawings, and photographs.

Here are some of the features of DALL-E Playground:

- It is easy to use. Simply type a text description of the image you want to create and DALL-E will generate an image based on your description.

- It is powerful. DALL-E can create realistic images from a wide variety of text descriptions.

- It is creative. DALL-E can generate images that are both original and visually appealing.

- It is fun. DALL-E Playground is a great way to experiment with AI and to create new and interesting images.

If you are interested in learning more about DALL-E Playground, you can visit the DALL-E Playground website. You can also find a tutorial on how to use DALL-E Playground on the OpenAI website.

Example: Generated Image with Promote: Multiple Northern Light

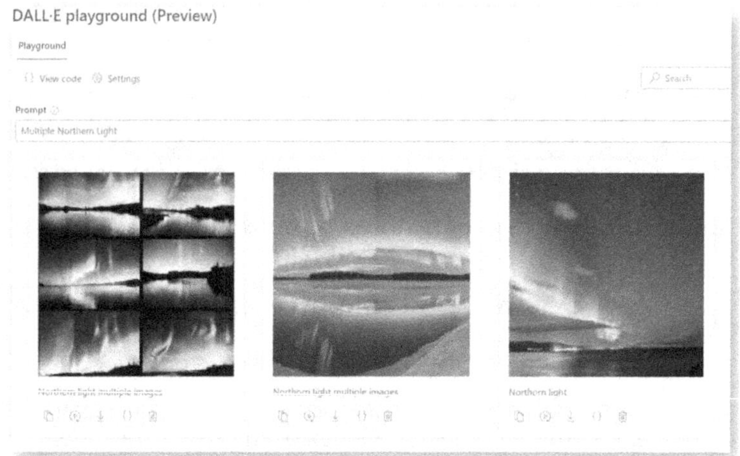

Section 7.7: Call Azure OpenAI Model to your custom program using API

Example Azure OpenAI API:

However, if you want to call an OpenAI language model using Python and generate text based on a prompt related to the Fibonacci series, you can follow these general steps:

1. **Install the OpenAI package:** Use pip or conda to install the OpenAI Python package by running the following command: pip install OpenAI

2. **Set up OpenAI credentials:** Obtain your OpenAI API key from the OpenAI website. Once you have your API

key, you need to set it as an environment variable in your Python script. You can do this by using the following code snippet:

```
import os

os.environ["OPENAI_API_KEY"] = "YOUR_API_KEY"
```

3. Create a function to generate text: Write a function that uses the OpenAI API to generate text based on a prompt related to the Fibonacci series. For example, you can provide a prompt like "Generate the Fibonacci series up to 10 numbers." Use the openai.Completion.create() method to send the prompt to the OpenAI API and receive the generated text.

4. The API response is stored in the response variable, and we extract the generated text from response.choices[0].text. We remove any leading or trailing whitespace using strip().

Call the function and print the generated text: Use the function you created to generate text based on a prompt related to the Fibonacci series. Here's an example:

```python
import openai

import os


# Set up OpenAI credentials

openai.api_key = os.getenv("OPENAI_API_KEY")


def generate_fibonacci_text(prompt):

    response = openai.Completion.create(

        engine="davinci-codex",

        prompt=prompt,

        max_tokens=100,

        temperature=0.7,

        n=1,

        stop=None,

        timeout=10

    )


    return response.choices[0].text.strip()


# Define the prompt

prompt = "Generate the Fibonacci series up to 10 numbers."


# Generate text based on the prompt

generated_text = generate_fibonacci_text(prompt)


# Print the generated text

print(generated_text)
```

Section 7.8: Best practices for effectively using Azure OpenAI as a developer

1. **Understand the OpenAI Services:** Gain a clear understanding of the specific OpenAI services and APIs available within Azure. Familiarize yourself with their capabilities, limitations,

and use cases to choose the most appropriate service for your project.

2. **API Documentation:** Thoroughly review the API documentation provided by Azure OpenAI. Understand how to make API calls, handle authentication, and interpret the responses. This will help you effectively interact with the services.

3. **Use Sandbox/Test Environments:** Before deploying in production, utilize sandbox or test environments to experiment, develop, and fine-tune your applications. This ensures that your code works as expected and helps avoid unexpected issues.

4. **Optimize Inputs:** Structure your input data appropriately for the specific OpenAI service you are using. Ensure that the input data is formatted correctly and contains relevant information for accurate results.

5. **Manage Authentication:** Follow secure authentication practices when interacting with Azure OpenAI APIs. Use API keys or tokens as recommended by Azure, and avoid hardcoding sensitive information in your code.

6. **Error Handling:** Implement robust error handling mechanisms in your code. Handle API errors gracefully by

checking response status codes and handling exceptions to prevent crashes and unexpected behavior.

7. **Monitor and Analyze:** Regularly monitor your applications that use Azure OpenAI services. Set up logging and monitoring tools to track usage, performance, and potential issues. Use these insights to optimize your applications.

8. **Data Privacy and Security:** Ensure that the data you provide to OpenAI services adheres to privacy and security standards. Be cautious while sharing sensitive or personally identifiable information.

9. **Scalability:** Design your applications with scalability in mind. Consider how your application will handle increased usage and traffic, and implement strategies to scale resources as needed.

10. **Stay Updated:** Keep up-to-date with the latest developments, updates, and improvements in Azure OpenAI services. Regularly check for new features, best practices, and any changes in APIs or usage guidelines.

11. **Cost Management:** Be mindful of the cost associated with using Azure OpenAI services. Monitor usage and set budget thresholds to avoid unexpected expenses.

12. **Community and Support:** Engage with the Azure and OpenAI communities to seek help, share experiences, and stay informed. Utilize available support channels and resources provided by Azure for assistance.

Section 7.9: Comprehensive documentation and resources for Azure OpenAI

You can find comprehensive documentation and resources for Azure OpenAI on the official Microsoft Azure website. Here are the steps to access the documentation:

1. Visit the Azure Documentation Website: Go to the Microsoft Azure documentation website at https://docs.microsoft.com/en-us/azure/.

2. Search for OpenAI: In the search bar at the top of the page, type "Azure OpenAI" or the specific OpenAI service you are interested in, such as "Azure Cognitive Services" or "Azure Machine Learning."

3. Select Documentation: Click on the relevant search result to access the documentation for Azure OpenAI services. The documentation will provide detailed information, tutorials, guides, sample code, and best practices for using Azure OpenAI services effectively.

4. Explore Additional Resources: In addition to the official documentation, you can also explore related resources such as blogs, videos, webinars, and community forums to learn more about Azure OpenAI and stay updated on the latest developments.

5. Azure Portal: You can also find information about Azure OpenAI within the Azure portal itself. Log in to the Azure portal (https://portal.azure.com/) and navigate to the "AI + Machine Learning" or relevant sections to access information about OpenAI services, APIs, and deployment options.

Chapter 8

LLM, GPT Model
Architecture and Training (4 hours)

Section 8.1 What is LLM

LLM stands for Large Language Model. It is a type of artificial intelligence (AI) that has been trained on a massive dataset of text and code. This allows it to generate text, translate languages, write different kinds of creative content, and answer your questions in an informative way.

LLMs are still under development, but they have the potential to revolutionize the way we interact with computers. They can be used to create more natural and engaging user interfaces, to generate more creative and informative content, and to automate tasks that are currently done by humans.

Here are some examples of how LLMs are being used today:

- Generating text: LLMs can be used to generate text for a variety of purposes, such as writing news articles, creating marketing copy, or generating creative content like poems, code, scripts, musical pieces, email, letters, etc.

- Translating languages: LLMs can be used to translate text from one language to another with a high degree of accuracy. This can be useful for businesses that need to communicate with customers or partners in other countries.

- Writing different kinds of creative content: LLMs can be used to write different kinds of creative content, such as poems, stories, scripts, and musical pieces. This can be useful for businesses that need to create marketing materials or for individuals who want to express themselves creatively.

- Answering your questions in an informative way: LLMs can be used to answer your questions in an informative way, even if they are open ended, challenging, or strange. This can be useful for students who need help with their homework or for people who want to learn more about a particular topic.

LLMs are a powerful new tool that has the potential to change the way we interact with computers. As they continue to develop, we can expect to see even more innovative and creative applications for this technology.

LLM Examples

- GPT-3 (Generative Pretrained Transformer 3): Developed by OpenAI, GPT-3 is one of the most well-known LLMs. It has over 175 billion parameters and can be used for a variety of tasks, including generating text, translating languages, and writing different kinds of creative content.

- BERT (Bidirectional Encoder Representations from Transformers): Developed by Google, BERT is another popular LLM. It is smaller than GPT-3, with only 110 million parameters, but it is still very effective for a variety of tasks, including natural language understanding and question answering.

- Turing NLG (Natural Language Generation): Developed by Microsoft, Turing NLG is an LLM that is specifically designed for generating text. It can be used to create realistic and engaging text for a variety of purposes, such as news articles, marketing copy, and creative content.

- LaMDA (Language Model for Dialogue Applications): Developed by Google, LaMDA is an LLM that is specifically designed for generating conversation. It can be used to create chatbots that can have natural and engaging conversations with humans.

These are just a few examples of the many LLMs that are available today. As LLM technology continues to develop, we can expect to see even more powerful and versatile LLMs that can be used for a wider range of tasks.

Section 8.2 How Architecture of GPT models work

1. The architecture of GPT (Generative Pre-trained Transformer) models is based on the transformer architecture, which is a neural network architecture designed for processing sequential data like text. The key components of the GPT architecture are as follows:

1. **Transformer Architecture:** GPT models use a variant of the transformer architecture, which consists of an encoder-decoder structure. In the case of GPT, only the decoder part is used, as the model is designed for autoregressive language generation.

2. **Self-Attention Mechanism:** Self-attention is a crucial component of the transformer architecture. It allows

the model to weigh the importance of different words in a sentence with respect to each other, capturing long-range dependencies. GPT models use multi-head self-attention, enabling them to focus on different aspects of the input text.

3. **Positional Encodings:** Since transformers do not inherently understand the order of words in a sequence, positional encodings are added to the input embeddings. These encodings provide the model with information about the position of each word in the sequence.

4. **Layer Stacking:** GPT models consist of multiple layers of self-attention and feedforward neural networks. These layers are stacked on top of each other, enabling the model to capture complex patterns and relationships in the input text.

5. **Feedforward Neural Networks:** Each layer in the GPT model contains a feedforward neural network, which helps in learning context-based representations of words.

6. **Masked Self-Attention:** During training, GPT models use a masked self-attention mechanism where each

position in the sequence can only attend to previous positions. This ensures that the model doesn't have access to future information during autoregressive text generation.

7. **Position-wise Feedforward Networks:** After the self-attention layer, a position-wise feedforward network is applied to each position independently. This network consists of a fully connected layer followed by a non-linear activation function.

8. **Layer Normalization and Residual Connections: Each** sub-layer (self-attention and feedforward) is followed by layer normalization and a residual connection. These mechanisms help in stabilizing and accelerating training.

9. **Embedding Layer:** Input tokens are initially embedded into continuous vector representations. In GPT, a learned embedding matrix is used to represent each token.

The architecture's autoregressive nature means that during text generation, the model predicts one token at a time while conditioning on the previously generated tokens. GPT models are trained on massive amounts of text data using unsupervised learning, learning to predict the next word in a sequence. This enables them to generate coherent and contextually relevant text based on the provided prompts.

Overall, the architecture of GPT models, particularly their utilization of the transformer architecture and self-attention mechanisms, allows them to capture intricate language patterns and generate human-like text sequences.

Section 8.2.1 GPT Architecture

A chat-based GPT model architecture is an extension of the standard GPT architecture, tailored for conversational interactions. Here's a textual description of the architecture:

1. **Input Encoding:** The conversation history, including user messages and model-generated responses, is tokenized and encoded. Each token is transformed into a vector representation using an embedding layer.

2. **Positional Encodings:** Just like in the standard GPT architecture, positional encodings are added to the token embeddings to indicate the order of tokens in the sequence.

3. **Transformer Layers:** The conversation history embeddings pass through multiple transformer layers. Each layer contains a multi-head self-attention

mechanism followed by position-wise feedforward neural networks.

4. **Contextual Information:** The self-attention mechanism helps the model capture contextual information from the conversation history, enabling it to understand the relationship between different messages.

5. **Response Generation:** After processing the conversation history, the model generates a response token by token. Autoregressive sampling is typically used, where the model generates one token at a time based on the previously generated tokens.

6. **Temperature and Top-k Sampling:** During response generation, parameters like temperature and top-k sampling can be adjusted to influence the creativity and randomness of the generated responses.

7. **Output Decoding:** The response tokens generated by the model are decoded using the model's vocabulary to generate human-readable text.

8. **Back-and-Forth Interaction:** This process can be repeated for multiple turns of conversation. The model

takes the entire conversation history into account to generate contextually relevant responses.

It's important to note that the architecture can vary based on the specific implementation and model version. GPT models, including chat-based ones, are pretrained on massive datasets using unsupervised learning. This allows them to capture language patterns, context, and generate coherent and contextually relevant responses in conversations.

For a visual representation of the architecture, I recommend referring to the official OpenAI documentation or research papers, which might include diagrams to illustrate the architecture.

Chapter 9

Prompt Engineering

Section 9.1 What is Prompt Engineering

Prompt engineering is the process of crafting prompts that are used to control the output of a large language model (LLM). A prompt is a short piece of text that provides the LLM with instructions on what to do. For example, a prompt could be "Write a poem about a cat" or "Translate this sentence from English to French."

1. In the context of models like GPT, prompt engineering involves considering factors like:

1. **Clarity:** Prompts should be clear and concise, providing a specific direction to the model about the desired output. Ambiguities or vague phrasing in prompts can lead to unpredictable or incorrect responses.

2. **Context:** Depending on the task, providing relevant context in the prompt can help the model understand

the context of the conversation and generate more contextually appropriate responses.

3. **Examples:** Providing examples of the desired output format or style can guide the model to generate responses that match the provided examples.

4. **Formatting:** For tasks involving structured output (e.g., code generation), including specific formatting instructions in the prompt can help the model produce the desired format.

5. **Temperature and Sampling:** For creative tasks, adjusting parameters like temperature and sampling techniques in the prompt can influence the randomness and creativity of the generated content.

6. **Bias and Sensitivity:** Prompt engineering can be used to guide the model to avoid generating biased, sensitive, or inappropriate content.

7. **Steerability:** Prompts can be designed to steer the model's output in a specific direction, allowing users to control the content generated by the model more effectively.

8. **Length Control:** When generating text of a specific length, prompts can include instructions to ensure the model produces output of the desired length.

Here are some examples of prompt engineering:

- **Adding context:** Prompt engineers can add context to a prompt by providing the LLM with additional information about the topic or task at hand. For example, a prompt for a poem about a cat could be "Write a poem about a cat that is lost in the woods."

- **Using keywords:** Prompt engineers can use keywords to help the LLM focus on specific aspects of a task. For example, a prompt for a translation from English to French could be "Translate this sentence from English to French: 'I love you.'"

- **Asking questions:** Prompt engineers can ask questions to the LLM to get it to generate specific outputs. For example, a prompt for a creative writing prompt could be "Write a story about a character who is lost in an Amazon Forest."

Effective prompt engineering requires an understanding of the language model's capabilities and limitations. Experimenting with different prompts and strategies is often necessary to find the best approach for a given task. As AI models continue to improve, prompt engineering becomes an essential skill for obtaining accurate and reliable results from these models.

Examples of prompt engineering techniques for GPT models?

1. Prompt engineering is about giving the model clear instructions and examples to help it understand what we want it to do.

2. We **describe the task and how to solve it,** so the model knows what we're asking for.

3. We also show the **model examples of correct answers to guide** it in providing the right results.

GPT Chat – Uses GPT-35-Turbo

Consist of Following :

1.System : What role AI to play

2.User: Prompt.

3.Assistance: Provide answer based on the prompt

Example #1

System:

You are an AI assistant that helps people find information.

User : Write an introduction for a weekly newsletter. -- Prompt

Assistance: Welcome to our weekly newsletter! We're thrilled to have you as a subscriber and look forward to sharing the latest news, insights, and tips with you. Each week, we'll be curating a collection of articles, interviews, and resources that we think you'll find valuable. Our goal is to provide you with the information you need to stay up-to-date on

User : Summarize it my 6 years old can understand – Prompt

Assistance : The newsletter says "welcome" and will share cool stuff every week to help you learn new things and be better at stuff.

Section 9.2 Prompt Engineering - What is In-Context and Shots

"In-context" and "Shots" are concepts related to OpenAI's approach to prompting and controlling the output of its language models like GPT-3 and GPT-4.

In-Context:

"In-context" refers to providing the language model with relevant and specific information before generating the output. It involves giving the model a context or background information to ensure that the generated text is coherent and relevant to the given context. This is particularly important when generating text that should follow a specific topic or style. By providing context, the model can better understand the user's intent and generate more accurate and appropriate responses.

Shots:

"Shots" are a way to control the behavior of the language model by specifying how many times it should be given new instructions or "shots" of input. Each shot contains the prompt and additional information that guides the model's generation. By using multiple shots, users can provide step-by-step instructions or influence the model's output in a more directed manner. This approach allows for more interactive and controlled conversations with the model.

Both in-context and shots are techniques that contribute to prompt engineering, helping users get the desired outputs from language models while maintaining control over the generated content. They are particularly useful in scenarios where precise control and tailored responses are required.

In-context :

In an In-Context learning process models are given the **natural language/ text instruction and based** on the text instruction on model process the steps and following

Three types : Few Shot , One-Shot ,Zero-Shot

Few-Shot: Multiple examples are provided

One-Shot : Only one example is provided

Zero-Shot : No example provided

Prompt:

Extract the name and mailing address from this email:

Dear Bob,

It was a nice conversation

.

Here's my address 3111 Lusk Blvd, San Diego CA 92126

Best,

Ak

Completion:

Name: AK

Mailing Address: 3111 Lusk Blvd, San Diego CA 92126

Section 9.3 Prompt Engineering – Text Classification

Text classification in prompt engineering refers to the process of categorizing or labeling text data into predefined classes or categories. It involves training a machine learning model to recognize patterns and features in text that differentiate one category from another. This trained model can then be used to automatically classify new, unseen text data into the appropriate categories.

In the context of prompt engineering, text classification is often used to guide the behavior of language models like GPT when generating responses. By providing a classification label as part of the prompt, you can instruct the model to generate text that is relevant to a specific category or topic. This helps in tailoring the output of the language model to align with a particular theme or intent.

For example, if you want to use a language model to generate product descriptions, you can provide a classification label indicating the product category (e.g., electronics, fashion, food). The model can then generate text that is appropriate for that category, resulting in more relevant and coherent responses.

Text classification is a powerful technique in prompt engineering as it allows you to exert fine-grained control over the generated content by explicitly specifying the desired category or context for the text generation process.

194

Text classification

Custom Named Entities (Few-Shot)

Prompt:

Sentence: John has been working for Microsoft for 10 years as a Software Engineer.

Job title: Software Engineer

###

Sentence: John has been working for Microsoft for 10 years he likes his job.

Job title: none

Multi-Label Text Classification (Few-Shot)

Prompt:

The following is a list of movies and the categories they fall into:

1.   Inception: A skilled thief who enters people's dreams to steal information finds himself involved in a dangerous plot that goes beyond anything he could have imagined.

Category: Science Fiction, Action, Thriller

2. The Notebook: A young couple's passionate and tumultuous love story is told through the eyes of an older man reflecting on his past.

Category: Romance, Drama

Paraphrase

Preface

Prompt:

Article: Renewable energy sources like solar and wind power are crucial for reducing carbon emissions and mitigating the impact of climate change.

Completion :

Paraphrase:

Renewable energy sources such as solar and wind power play a critical role in decreasing carbon emissions and addressing the consequences of climate change.

Multi-Label Text Classification (Few-Shot)

Prompt:

The following is a list of movies and the categories they fall into:

The Avengers: Earth's mightiest heroes come together to form a team and save the world from a powerful threat. Category:

Category: Action, Adventure, Science Fiction

Keyword Extraction

Prompt:

Extract Key word from the sentence

 Assessing key phrase effectiveness: Using familiar content to determine the level of understanding conveyed by the generated key phrases.

Completion :

Keyword: document, understand, key phrases

Summarize of contact center

Prompt :

Summarize this for a call center agent:

Agent: Thank you for contacting XYZ Corporation. May I know who I am speaking with?

 Customer: Hi, my name is Sarah Johnson. I have a few questions regarding our company's IT infrastructure.

Agent: Good morning, Sarah. Before we proceed, may I ask you a few questions to better assist you today?

Customer: That would be great. Are there any specific security measures we need to implement?

 Agent: Yes, certain aspects of IT security are regulated by industry standards and compliance requirements.

Completion: The agent is speaking to a customer named Sarah Johnson. Sarah is seeking guidance on IT infrastructure. The agent informs Sarah that certain aspects of IT security are regulated by industry standards and compliance requirements.

Prompt Insert

These are agenda topics for a customer presentation.

1. New Product Launch

[insert]

10. Conclusion

These are agenda topics for a customer presentation.

1. Introduction and Welcome
2. Company Overview
3. Market Analysis and Trends
4. Problem Statement and Customer Needs
5. Solution Overview: New Product Launch
6. Key Features and Benefits
7. Use Cases and Demonstrations
8. Pricing and Packaging
9. Implementation and Onboarding Process
10. Customer Testimonials
11. Success Stories and Case Studies
12. Conclusion and Next Steps
13. Q&A Session
14. Closing Remarks
15. Conclusion

[human]: Hi there! How are you doing?

[robot]: Hello! I'm doing well, thank you. How about you?

[human]: I'm feeling a bit overwhelmed with work lately.

[robot]: I understand. Work can sometimes be demanding. Is there anything specific that's causing the overwhelm? [

human]: I have multiple deadlines to meet and it's stressing me out.

[robot]: I can imagine. It's important to take breaks and prioritize tasks. Is there anything I can do to assist you in managing your workload?

[human]: Just having someone to talk to about it helps. Thank you for listening.

Product recommendation (Few-Shot)

Generate product recommendations:

Product: shoes, shirt, hat

Recommendation: sunglasses

Product: laptop, tablet, smartphone Recommendation: headphones

Product: camera, tripod, lens

Recommendation: Camera Bag

Section 9.4 Prompt Engineering – Special Separation

Special Separation (---)

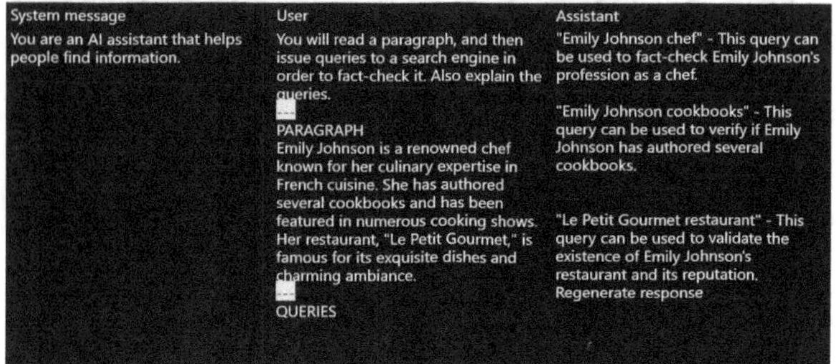

Section 9.5 Prompt Engineering – Chain of Thoughts

A "chain of thoughts" refers to a sequence of prompts that are strategically designed to guide the output of a language model like GPT. This sequence of prompts is crafted in such a way that the model's responses build upon each other, creating a coherent and contextually relevant flow of information.

The idea behind a chain of thoughts is to provide the language model with a context that it can use to generate responses that are consistent and connected. Each prompt in the chain sets the stage for the subsequent prompts, allowing the model to generate text that follows a logical progression of ideas.

For example, if you're using GPT to write a story, you can create a chain of thoughts like this:

Prompt 1: "Once upon a time, in a small village, there lived a young girl named Emily."

Prompt 2: "Emily had a curious nature and a love for exploring the woods near her village."

Prompt 3: "One day, while venturing deep into the woods, Emily stumbled upon an ancient-looking map."

In this example, each prompt adds to the narrative, and the model's responses are expected to follow the storyline established by the previous prompts. By carefully constructing a chain of thoughts, you can guide the language model's creativity while ensuring that the generated content remains coherent and contextually appropriate.

Chain of thoughts is a technique that leverages the model's ability to build upon previous prompts, enabling you to create more structured and engaging interactions with the language model.

Example Chain of Thoughts:

System message	User	Assistant
You are an AI assistant that helps people find information.	Who was the most famous actress in Hollywood between year 1960 to 1990 Take a step-by-step approach in your response, cite sources, and give reasoning before sharing the final answer in the below format: ANSWER is: <name>	Step 1: Define the criteria for "famous action actor." Specify the criteria for fame and action-oriented roles, considering factors such as popularity, iconic performances in action films, box office success, critical acclaim, and lasting influence on the genre. Final Answer: ANSWER is: [Name of the actor] is widely considered the most famous action actor in Hollywood between the years 1960 to 1990. He achieved immense success and recognition for his action films, including [mention specific iconic action movies]. His performances captivated audiences, and his contributions to the action genre continue to resonate in the industry.

Section 9.6 Prompt Engineering - Prompt Chucking:

Prompt chunking is a technique used in prompt engineering to break down a complex query or instruction into smaller, more manageable parts or "chunks" before presenting them to a language model like GPT. The goal of prompt chunking is to improve the model's understanding of the input and generate more accurate and contextually relevant responses.

When a prompt is too long or complex, language models may struggle to comprehend the entirety of the input and generate coherent output. By breaking the prompt into smaller chunks, each containing a specific piece of information or instruction, you make it easier for the model to process and respond effectively.

For example, consider a complex prompt for a language model:

Complex Prompt: "Translate the following English text into French: 'The quick brown fox jumps over the lazy dog'."

In this case, prompt chunking might involve breaking down the instruction into smaller parts:

Chunked Prompts:

1. "Translate the following English text into French:"

2. "'The quick brown fox jumps over the lazy dog'."

By presenting the instruction in smaller chunks, you help the language model focus on one aspect at a time, reducing the chances of misinterpretation and improving the quality of the generated response.

Prompt chunking is particularly useful when working with language models to ensure that they correctly understand and respond to each element of a prompt, especially when dealing with multi-step instructions or complex queries. It enhances the model's ability to process and generate accurate content, ultimately leading to better outcomes in various tasks.

Example Prompt Chucking:

> **Prompt :** Please divide the original prompt into smaller chunks focusing on different aspects of renewable energy. I would like separate prompts for environmental benefits, economic feasibility, and long-term sustainability."
>
> Original Prompt:
>
> "Write a persuasive essay arguing for the implementation of renewable energy sources as the primary energy solution for combating climate change. Include evidence on the environmental benefits, economic feasibility, and long-term sustainability of renewable energy."
>
> Assistance :
>
> Prompt Chunking:
>
> Prompt Chunk 1: "Write a persuasive essay arguing for the implementation of renewable energy sources as the primary energy solution for combating climate change."
>
> Prompt Chunk 2: "Include evidence on the environmental benefits of renewable energy."
>
> Prompt Chunk 3: "Include evidence on the economic feasibility of renewable energy."

Prompt Engineering – Best Practices

Prompt engineering is a crucial aspect of working with language models like GPT to achieve desired outputs. Here are some best practices for effective prompt engineering:

1. Be Clear and Specific: Write prompts that clearly convey the context and desired output. The model's response is based on the information in the prompt, so clarity is key.

2. Use Complete Sentences: Formulate prompts as complete sentences to provide clear context and minimize ambiguity.

3. Provide Examples: Include examples of the desired response format to guide the model. You can use explicit instruction, like "In three sentences, explain...".

4. Experiment with Different Prompts: Try various prompts to see how the model responds. Sometimes slight rephrasing can yield better results.

5. Steer the Model: Use explicit instructions to guide the model's behavior. For instance, you can say "Contrast the advantages and disadvantages of..." to prompt a balanced response.

6. Temperature and Max Tokens: Adjust the temperature parameter to control the randomness of the output. Set max tokens to limit the length of the response.

7. Incorporate Context: Use the "In-context" feature to refer to previous model responses. This helps maintain context in ongoing conversations.

8. Consider Shots: Shots allow you to have multiple back-and-forth with the model within a single call.

9. Avoid Open-Ended Prompts: For focused results, avoid overly open-ended prompts. Instead, provide specific instructions.

10. Prompt Chunking: Break down complex requests into smaller, manageable chunks.

11. Regular Testing: Continuously test and iterate your prompts to refine the quality of the model's responses.

12. Feedback Loop: If you're using the model for a specific task, iteratively improve your prompts based on the model's responses and user feedback.

13. Use Affordances: Utilize affordances to guide the model's behavior by instructing it to think from a particular perspective.

14. Understand Model Capabilities: Familiarize yourself with what the model can and cannot do. This helps in crafting realistic prompts.

15. Prioritize Ethical Use: Avoid generating harmful, offensive, or inappropriate content by being mindful of your prompts.

16. Stay Updated: Keep up with updates and documentation from OpenAI to learn about new features and best practices.

Remember that prompt engineering is an iterative process. Experiment, learn from the model's responses, and refine your prompts accordingly. It's important to balance creativity with clear communication to get the best results.

Chapter 10

Content Filtering

Section 10.1: Content Filtering

Content filtering, also known as content moderation or content filtering, is the process of monitoring and controlling the information or content that is allowed to be accessed, shared, or displayed on a platform or system. Its primary purpose is to prevent the dissemination of inappropriate, offensive, harmful, or sensitive content that could be damaging to individuals or the platform itself.

Content filtering can be applied to various types of content, including text, images, videos, and more. It involves using automated tools, algorithms, or manual review processes to assess and categorize content based on predefined criteria. This criterion can include explicit language, explicit imagery, hate speech, violence, and other content that violates community guidelines or legal standards.

The main goals of content filtering:

1. Protect Users: Content filtering aims to provide a safe and positive user experience by preventing users from encountering harmful or inappropriate content.

2. Maintain Reputation: Platforms and websites want to maintain a positive reputation and create a welcoming environment for their users. Effective content filtering helps in achieving this goal.

3. Compliance: In some cases, content filtering is necessary to ensure compliance with laws and regulations related to content, such as those addressing child exploitation, hate speech, and more.

4. Prevent Misuse: Content filtering can prevent the platform from being used for spam, scams, or other malicious activities.

5. User-Generated Content: Many platforms allow users to generate and share content. Content filtering helps ensure that user-generated content aligns with the platform's guidelines and values.

Content filtering methods can include:

- **Keyword Filtering:** Filtering content based on specific keywords or phrases that are flagged as inappropriate.

- **Image Recognition:** Analyzing images and videos for explicit or sensitive content.

-**Text Analysis:** Analyzing text content for hate speech, profanity, or other violations.

- **Machine Learning:** Using machine learning algorithms to identify patterns in content that may indicate inappropriate material.

-**User Reporting:** Allowing users to report content that they find inappropriate, which can then be reviewed by moderators.

It's important to note that content filtering is not always perfect and can sometimes lead to false positives or false negatives. Striking the right balance between protecting users and allowing freedom of expression is a challenge. Additionally, content filtering should be implemented in a way that respects users' privacy and doesn't unnecessarily infringe on their rights.

SUMMARY & CONCLUSION- PRPOMPT ENGINEERING & CONTENT FILTERING

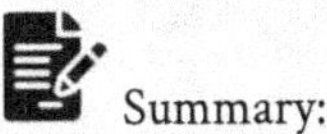 Summary:

Prompt Engineering:

Prompt engineering involves crafting well-structured and specific prompts to guide AI models' responses. It aims to optimize the output quality by providing clear context, instructions, and relevant information in prompts. Effective prompt engineering enhances the model's ability to understand and generate accurate and desired content.

Content Filtering:

Content filtering involves implementing mechanisms to monitor, moderate, or restrict the content generated by AI models. It aims to prevent the generation of inappropriate, offensive, or harmful content. Content filtering is crucial to ensure that AI-generated outputs align with ethical and regulatory standards.

Conclusion: In the world of AI, effective prompt engineering is essential for guiding models like Codex to produce accurate and desired results. Properly structured prompts enhance communication between humans and AI, resulting in improved outcomes. However, content filtering remains a vital consideration to prevent undesirable content generation and maintain ethical usage of AI models.

Note In summary, prompt engineering and content filtering collectively contribute to harnessing the potential of AI while ensuring responsible and ethical use. These practices empower users to interact effectively with AI models, leverage code generation capabilities, and maintain a safe and respectful AI environment.

CHAPTER 10 QUIZ: TEST YOUR SKILLS

Prompt Engineering:

1. What is the primary goal of prompt engineering in language models?

    a) Enhancing dataset diversity

    b) Fine-tuning model parameters

    c) Improving natural language understanding

    d) Increasing model training time

2. In prompt engineering, what is "in-context" used to refer to?

    a) Contextual understanding of user input

    b) Prompts written in a formal tone

    c) Irrelevant data points in training

    d) Inadequate prompt examples

3. What is the purpose of "shots" in prompt engineering?

    a) Rapid model training

    b) Including images in prompts

    c) Boosting model performance

    d) Generating longer text outputs

4. Which of the following is a technique used in prompt engineering for text classification?

a) Code generation

b) Content filtering

c) Data visualization

d) Audio transcription

5. How does prompt chunking contribute to prompt engineering?

a) Organizing prompts into manageable sections

b) Increasing the token limit for a single prompt

c) Removing contextual information from prompts

d) Merging multiple prompts into one

Content Filtering:

6. What is the main purpose of content filtering in online platforms?

a) Maximizing user engagement

b) Ensuring quality content is highlighted

c) Identifying and removing inappropriate or harmful content

d) Promoting controversial discussions

7. How does content filtering contribute to user safety?

a) It exposes users to diverse opinions

b) It prevents users from accessing any content

c) It reduces exposure to harmful or misleading content

d) It only allows verified users to post content

8. What are "blacklists" and "whitelists" commonly used for in content filtering?

a) Organizing content by popularity

b) Categorizing content by color

c) Identifying trusted and blocked content sources

d) Ranking content based on relevance

9. Why is fine-tuning important in content filtering?

a) It increases the amount of content displayed to users

b) It helps adjust the filter's sensitivity to avoid false positives and negatives

c) It speeds up the loading of web pages

d) It makes the filtering process completely automatic

CHAPERT 10 QUIZ: ASWER

Prompt Engineering:

1. Answer: c) Improving natural language understanding

2. Answer: a) Contextual understanding of user input

3. Answer: c) Boosting model performance

4. Answer: b) Content filtering

5. Answer: a) Organizing prompts into manageable sections

Content Filtering:

6. Answer: c) Identifying and removing inappropriate or harmful content

7. Answer: c) It reduces exposure to harmful or misleading content

8. Answer: c) Identifying trusted and blocked content sources

9. Answer: b) It helps adjust the filter's sensitivity to avoid false positives and negatives

Please note that the answers are based on the context provided in the questions.

Chapter 11

Hallucination & Fine Tuning

Section 11.1 Hallucination

In the context of language models like GPT (Generative Pre-trained Transformer), "hallucination" refers to the phenomenon where the model generates text that is creative or imaginative but not necessarily grounded in reality or factual information. It can produce sentences or paragraphs that seem coherent and plausible on the surface but are not accurate or true in the real world.

Hallucination occurs when the model generates text that goes beyond its training data and generates content that may sound convincing but lacks actual factual basis. This can happen because the model has learned patterns and associations from the training data that it then extrapolates to generate new content, even if that content is not supported by facts.

For example, a GPT-based model might generate a story that includes fictional events, characters, or details that are not present in the training data. While this creativity can be beneficial for tasks like creative writing, it can also lead to the generation of misinformation or inaccuracies.

Controlling and minimizing hallucination is an ongoing challenge in natural language generation, especially when the model is generating content beyond its training data. Researchers and developers continually work on improving models' ability to generate coherent and contextually relevant text while maintaining accuracy and truthfulness.

Examples:

Sure, here are some examples of hallucination generated by language models like GPT:

1. **Historical Events:** "In the year 1925, Albert Einstein invented a time machine and traveled to the future to meet Steve Jobs."

2. **Scientific Claims:** "According to a recent study, humans can communicate telepathically with dolphins using a special frequency."

3. **Fictional Facts:** "In the Harry Potter universe, the spell 'Luminos' can actually light up real-life rooms."

4. **Unverified Information:** "Studies have shown that eating three chocolate bars a day can improve your IQ by 50 points."

5. Implausible Scenarios: "Last week, a flying elephant was spotted over New York City, causing traffic jams and excitement among citizens."

These examples showcase how language models can generate text that is imaginative but not based on factual information. While such creativity can be entertaining, it's important to distinguish between factual and fictional content, especially when considering information for educational, informative, or decision-making purposes.

Best Practices for Hallucination

When working with language models to generate text, including potential hallucinations, it's important to ensure that the output aligns with the intended purpose and context. Here are some best practices for handling hallucination or imaginative content responsibly:

1. Clearly Label Fictional Content: If you're sharing text that includes imaginative or fictional information, make sure to clearly label it as such. This helps readers differentiate between factual and creative content.

2. Provide Context: Whenever presenting hallucinatory content, provide sufficient context to indicate that it's not based on real-world facts. Avoid presenting it as genuine information, especially in serious or informative contexts.

3. Educational and Entertainment Use: Use hallucination responsibly in educational or entertainment contexts, such as creative writing, storytelling, or generating fictional scenarios for fun.

4. Avoid Misinformation: Ensure that any hallucinatory content does not promote false or misleading information that could be harmful or misinterpreted.

5. Engage Audience Appropriately: Know your audience and tailor the use of hallucination accordingly. For educational purposes, clearly state that the content is imaginative and not factual.

6. Fact-Check and Verify: If you're presenting any information, even imaginative, ensure that it doesn't conflict with established facts. It's important to maintain credibility and avoid spreading false information.

7. Use Descriptive Warnings: If sharing hallucinatory content, include clear disclaimers or warnings that help readers understand the content's nature and purpose.

8. Encourage Critical Thinking: When presenting imaginative content, encourage your audience to engage in critical thinking and question the plausibility of the information.

Remember that while hallucination can be a creative and engaging way to use language models, responsible usage is key to maintaining trust and preventing the spread of misinformation.

Fine Tuning

Chapter 11.2: Fine Tuning

Section 11.2: What is Fine Tuning

Fine-tuning in the context of language models like GPT (Generative Pre-trained Transformer) refers to the process of further training a pre-trained model on a specific dataset to adapt it for a particular task or domain. The idea behind fine-tuning is to take a pre-trained model that has learned a wide range of language understanding and generation capabilities and specialize it to perform better on a specific task, such as text classification, sentiment analysis, question answering, or language translation.

Here's how the fine-tuning process generally works:

1. Pre-training: Initially, a language model like GPT is pre-trained on a massive dataset containing a diverse range of text from the internet. During pre-training, the model learns to predict the next word in a sentence, which helps it understand grammar, context, and general language patterns.

2. Fine-Tuning: After pre-training, the model can be fine-tuned on a smaller, task-specific dataset. This dataset is carefully curated to match the task you want the model to perform. Fine-tuning involves exposing the model to the new dataset and updating its parameters based on the specific patterns and requirements of the task.

3. Task-Specific Objectives: During fine-tuning, the model's training objectives are adjusted to suit the task. For example, if the task is sentiment analysis, the model might be trained to predict sentiment labels (positive, negative, neutral) based on text inputs.

4. Transfer Learning: Fine-tuning benefits from transfer learning, where the knowledge gained during pre-training is transferred to the task-specific domain. This is particularly useful when you have limited task-specific data.

5. Hyperparameter Tuning: Parameters like learning rate, batch size, and training epochs might need to be adjusted during fine-tuning to achieve optimal performance on the target task.

Fine-tuning allows you to leverage the general language understanding capabilities of a pre-trained model while tailoring it to your specific application. It can save training time and resources compared to training a language model from scratch. However, fine-tuning requires careful selection of the task-specific dataset, consideration of ethical implications, and monitoring of the model's outputs to ensure it behaves as desired.

Section 11.3: Fine Tuning Steps

Fine-tuning a language model like GPT involves several steps to adapt a pre-trained model for a specific task. Below is a general outline of the process:

1. Prepare Your Data:

- Gather and preprocess your task-specific dataset. This dataset should be relevant to the task you want the model to perform.

- Organize your data into a format suitable for training, including input text and corresponding labels if applicable.

2. Choose a Pre-trained Model:

- Select a pre-trained language model that aligns with the architecture and size you need. GPT-2, GPT-3, or other variants can be fine-tuned.

3. Install Required Libraries:

- Ensure you have the necessary Python libraries installed, such as TensorFlow, PyTorch, or Hugging Face Transformers.

4. Fine-Tuning Process:

- Load the pre-trained model of your choice using a library like Hugging Face Transformers.

- Modify the model's architecture or add task-specific layers if necessary.

- Use your prepared dataset to train the model. During training, you'll update the model's weights based on the task-specific data.

- Fine-tuning typically involves several epochs of training. You can experiment with hyperparameters like learning rate, batch size, and optimization algorithms to achieve the best results.

5. Validation and Evaluation:

- After each training epoch, validate the model's performance on a separate validation dataset to ensure it improving.

- Monitor metrics like accuracy, loss, or any relevant task-specific metrics.

6. Hyperparameter Tuning:

- Fine-tuning involves finding the right balance of hyperparameters. Experiment with different settings to achieve the best performance.

7. Save the Fine-Tuned Model:

- Once you're satisfied with the model's performance, save its weights and architecture.

8. Inference and Deployment:

- Load the fine-tuned model for inference on new data.

- Deploy the model in your desired environment, whether it's a web application, API, or any other platform where you want to use the model.

Remember that the fine-tuning process requires careful consideration of ethical concerns, especially when dealing with large language models. Fine-tuning can sometimes amplify biases present in the data, so it's crucial to monitor the model's behavior and address any potential issues.

It's also important to note that fine-tuning can be resource-intensive and might require access to substantial computational power and memory. Many open-source libraries provide tutorials and examples for fine-tuning, which can help you get started on the process.

Fine Tuning Best Practices

1. Model Selection: Choose a pre-trained model that suits your task and domain.

2. Quality Data: Use clean, relevant data for training that aligns with your task.

3. Validation and Testing: Set aside data for validation and testing to monitor model performance.

4. Learning Rate Scheduler: Implement a scheduler to gradually adjust the learning rate.

5. Monitor Metrics: Track evaluation metrics to gauge model progress and make informed decisions.

6. Regularization: Apply techniques like dropout and weight decay to prevent overfitting.

7. Ethical Considerations: Address biases and ethical concerns in your training data.

8. Documentation: Maintain detailed records for reproducibility and continuous improvement.

CHAPTER 11 QUIZ: TEST YOUR SKILL

Hallucination:

1. What is hallucination in the context of language models?

   a) Generating text that is coherent and factual

   b) Generating text that is accurate but lacks coherence

   c) Generating text that is factual but lacks context

   d) Generating text that seems coherent but is not grounded in facts

2. How can hallucination be mitigated in language models?

   a) By encouraging models to generate more creative content

   b) By ignoring factual accuracy and focusing on fluency

   c) By incorporating fact-checking mechanisms during training

   d) By intentionally introducing incorrect information in training data

Fine-tuning:

-3. What is fine-tuning in the context of language models?

   a) Refining the vocabulary used by the model

   b) Adjusting the model's hyperparameters during training

c) Adapting a pre-trained model to a specific task or domain

d) Converting textual input into numerical vectors

4. Which of the following is a benefit of fine-tuning a language model?

a) It reduces the need for pre-training

b) It improves the model's generalization to new tasks

c) It only works for tasks related to translation

d) It eliminates the need for labeled training data

General:

5. What is the primary purpose of text embedding?

a) Generating random text

b) Enhancing model creativity

c) Converting text into numerical representations

d) Adding formatting to text

6. How can hallucination in language models impact their usability?

a) It enhances the model's accuracy

b) It generates accurate but boring responses

c) It can lead to the generation of incorrect information

d) It only affects training performance

7. Which step is involved in fine-tuning a language model?

    a) Converting text to images

    b) Adapting the model to a specific task or domain

    c) Training the model from scratch

    d) Embedding images into the model

8. What does fine-tuning help achieve in language models?

    a) Overfitting to a specific task

    b) Generalizing across various tasks

    c) Eliminating the need for pre-training

    d) Generating longer and more complex text

9. What aspect of language models does hallucination detection focus on?

    a) Accurate grammar usage

    b) Coherent and contextually relevant responses

    c) Incorporating creative elements in the generated text

    d) Responding with longer and more detailed explanations

10. Why is text embedding important in NLP tasks?

    a) It replaces the need for machine learning models

    b) It makes text processing slower

    c) It transforms text into a format models can understand

    d) It reduces the complexity of language understanding

CHAPTER 11 QUIZ: ANSWERS

Hallucination:

1. d) Generating text that seems coherent but is not grounded in facts

2. c) By incorporating fact-checking mechanisms during training

Fine-tuning:

3. c) Adapting a pre-trained model to a specific task or domain

4. b) It improves the model's generalization to new tasks

General:

5. c) Converting text into numerical representations

6. c) It can lead to the generation of incorrect information

7. b) Adapting the model to a specific task or domain

8. b) Generalizing across various tasks

9. b) Coherent and contextually relevant responses

10. c) It transforms text into a format models can understand

SUMMARY & CONCLUSION- HALLUCINATION & FINE-TUNING

Summary:

1. **Hallucination:** Hallucination refers to a scenario where a language model generates text that seems coherent but is not grounded in factual information. It's important to recognize and address this issue during model training and deployment to ensure accurate and reliable responses.

2. **Fine-tuning:** Fine-tuning involves adapting a pre-trained language model to specific tasks or domains. It requires careful selection of training data, model architecture, and hyperparameters to achieve optimal performance on the target task.

Conclusion:

Hallucination detection, and fine-tuning are critical aspects of language model development and deployment. Detecting and mitigating hallucination ensures that the generated content is factually accurate. Fine-tuning adapts models to specific tasks, optimizing their performance. By incorporating these practices, developers can create powerful and reliable language models that deliver accurate and contextually relevant responses, meeting the demands of various applications while upholding ethical and factual standards.

Note Make sure to follow the proper guidelines/best practices for Embedding & Hallucination

Chapter 12

Use Cases [34]

**NOTE: All the use cases code download available :
https://github.com/books-code/books-openai.git**

Section 12.1: Installation Instructions

All the use cases are demonstrated here use Python and Streamlit. Here are the steps to install Python, Streamlit along with how to secure the access keys. You have option to use Azure OpenAI or OpenAI.

1. **Install Python**

    pip install python

 pip install streamlit openai

2.Example Steps for of calling an OpenAI model using Python and the OpenAI API

---

[34] NOTE : All the use cases code download available : https://github.com/books-code/books-openai.git

In this example, we use the OpenAI Python library to interact with the OpenAI API.

1. Install the OpenAI package: Use pip or condo to install the OpenAI Python package by running the following command:

Copy code

pip install openai

2.Set up OpenAI credentials: Obtain your OpenAI API key from the OpenAI website. Once you have your API key, you need to set it as an environment variable in your Python script. You can do this by using the following code snippet: **import os**

3.Add Authentication key:to authenticate the API

os.environ["OPENAI_API_KEY"] = "YOUR_API_KEY

4. Next, we define a prompt as the starting point for generating text. You can customize the promptbased on your specific use case.

5. Then, we make a call to the openai.Completion.create() method, specifying the engine (e.g., 'davinci') and the prompt. You can also set additional parameters like max_tokens to control the length of the generated text.

6. The API response is stored in the response variable, and we extract the generated text from response.choices[0].text. We remove any leading or trailing whitespace using strip().

7. Finally, we print the generated text to see the output of the OpenAI model.

Section12.1: Use Case # 1: Interview Question Generator [35]

Definition:

An Interview Question Generator is a tool or software that automatically generates a set of interview questions for various job positions and industries. It utilizes algorithms and data to create relevant and tailored questions that assess candidates' skills, knowledge, and suitability for a specific role.

Input:

- User Select Subject : User enter a subject such a Python /PHP/ C++ etc

- Number of Questions : between 1 to 20

Output :

---

[35] All the use cases code download available : https://github.com/books-code/books-openai.git

It generated 20 questions with answers

Software used:

- Python

- Streamlit

- OpeanAI /Azure OpenAI

Use Case #1:

The Interview Question Generator is widely used by HR professionals, recruiters, and hiring managers to streamline and enhance the interview process. Here's a use case scenario:

Scenario: A technology company is looking to hire a Software Engineer with expertise in machine learning. The HR team is tasked with creating a comprehensive set of interview questions that assess the candidates' technical skills, problem-solving abilities, and domain knowledge.

1. Problem Identification: The HR team defines the job requirements, technical skills, and qualifications needed for the Software Engineer role, including proficiency in machine learning algorithms and programming languages.

2. Input Data: The HR team inputs the job description, required qualifications, and specific technical skills into the Interview Question Generator.

3. Question Generation: The Interview Question Generator utilizes its algorithms to analyze the input data and generates a list of interview questions. These questions are designed to assess the candidate's understanding of machine learning concepts, coding skills, and problem-solving abilities.

4. Customization: The HR team reviews the generated questions and can further customize or fine-tune them based on the company's culture and specific requirements.

5. Interview Process: During the interview process, the generated questions are used to evaluate candidates' technical skills and fit for the role. The questions cover topics such as machine learning algorithms, data preprocessing, model evaluation, and programming tasks.

6. Candidate Assessment: The candidates' responses to the generated questions provide valuable insights into their level of expertise, thought process, and ability to apply theoretical knowledge to real-world scenarios.

Benefits:

- **Time Efficiency:** The Interview Question Generator saves time for HR teams by automating the process of creating tailored interview questions.

- **Consistency:** It ensures that all candidates are evaluated based on the same set of questions, promoting fairness and consistency in the hiring process.

- **Targeted Assessment:** The generated questions are closely aligned with the job requirements, enabling a more accurate assessment of candidates' suitability for the role.

- **Comprehensive Coverage:** It covers a wide range of topics and skills, ensuring that candidates are thoroughly evaluated from various angles.

- **Customization:** While generated questions are provided, the HR team can customize them to reflect the company's specific needs and values. in conclusion, an Interview Question Generator is a powerful tool that assists HR professionals in creating relevant and effective interview questions, enhancing the overall quality of the hiring process and facilitating the selection of qualified candidates.

USE CASE #1 Code: Interview Question Generator

 # START CODE

```python
import openai

import streamlit as st

import streamlit as st

import pandas as pd

import openai


# Set up OpenAI API

# Authenticate with OpenAI API

openai.api_type = "azure"

openai.api_base = 'https://testgptxxxxxxxx.openai.azure.com/'

openai.api_version = "2023-03-15-preview"

openai.api_key = 'xxxxxxxxxxxxxxxxxx'

#openai.api_key = st.secrets['path']

#model_engine = "text-davinci-003"

# Available GPT-3 models select which one you want to use

gpt3_models = [

 "text-davinci-003",

 "text-davinci-002",

 "gpt-35-turbo"

]

def generate_questions(subject, num_questions, temperature, max_tokens,
model_engine, question_level):
```

```python
prompt = f"Generate {num_questions} {question_level} level questions on {subject}\n"

response = openai.Completion.create(

engine=model_engine,

prompt=prompt,

max_tokens=max_tokens,

n=1,

stop=None,

temperature=temperature,

)

if response.choices[0].text:

result = response.choices[0].text.strip().split("\n")

questions = [q for q in result if "?" in q]

return questions

else:

return None

def main():

st.title("Question Generator")

# enter subjects such as Python or PHP etc.

subject = st.text_input("Enter a subject:")

# Total # of questions

num_questions = st.slider("Number of questions to generate", 1, 20, 10)

temperature = st.slider("Temperature", 0.1, 1.0, 0.5)
```

```python
max_tokens = st.slider("Max Tokens", 0, 8000, 100)

#Question Levels

question_level = st.selectbox("Select question level", ["Basic", "Medium",
"Advanced"])

question_level = question_level.lower()

model_engine = st.selectbox("Select GPT model", gpt3_models)

if st.button("Generate"):

questions = generate_questions(subject, num_questions, temperature,
max_tokens, model_engine, question_level)

if questions:

st.write("Generated Questions:")

for q in questions:

st.write(f"Q: {q}")

else:

st.write("No questions were generated.")

if __name__ == "__main__":

main()

# END OF THE CODE
```

Section 13.2 : USE CASE #2 : Stock Market Recommendations[36]

Definition:

A Stock Market Recommendations Use Case involves the application of data analysis, machine learning, and artificial intelligence to generate informed investment suggestions for buying, selling, or holding stocks in the financial market. This use case aims to assist investors, traders, and financial professionals in making well-informed decisions to optimize their investment portfolios.

Input :

- Enter : Stock Ticker Symbol

Output :

It generate recommendation

Software used :

- Python

- Streamlit

- OpeanAI /Azure OpenAI

---

[36] All the use cases code download available : https://github.com/books-code/books-openai.git

Use Case#2:

Scenario: An individual investor wants to make strategic investment decisions in the stock market to maximize returns while managing risks. They are looking for a solution that can provide personalized stock recommendations based on data-driven analysis and market trends.

1. Data Collection: The stock market recommendation system collects a vast amount of historical and real-time data, including stock prices, trading volumes, financial statements, news sentiment, economic indicators, and macroeconomic trends.

2. Data Preprocessing: The collected data is cleaned, transformed, and preprocessed to remove inconsistencies, handle missing values, and standardize formats. It is then organized into structured datasets suitable for analysis.

3. Feature Engineering: Relevant features are derived from the raw data to create indicators that represent market trends, financial ratios, technical analysis, and sentiment analysis.

4. Machine Learning Models: Various machine learning algorithms are applied to the preprocessed data to develop predictive models. These models use historical data to identify patterns, correlations, and trends that can guide future stock movements.

5. Recommendation Generation: Based on the trained models, the system generates personalized recommendations for stocks. These recommendations could include "Buy," "Sell," or "Hold" suggestions, along with predicted price targets and associated confidence levels.

6. Risk Assessment: The system also assesses the potential risks associated with each recommendation, considering factors such as volatility, market sentiment, and external events.

7. Real-time Updates: The system continuously monitors real-time market data and news updates. It adjusts its recommendations and predictions based on changing market conditions and events.

8. User Interface: Investors can access the recommendations through a user-friendly interface, which displays the suggested actions, rationale, risk analysis, and other relevant information.

Benefits:

- **Informed Decision-Making:** Investors receive data-backed stock recommendations, enabling them to make well-informed investment decisions aligned with their financial goals and risk tolerance.

- **Time Efficiency:** The use of machine learning accelerates the process of analyzing vast amounts of data, allowing investors to react quickly to market changes.

- **Personalization:** Recommendations are tailored to individual investor profiles, considering factors such as investment horizon, risk appetite, and financial objectives.

- **Risk Management:** The system assesses and communicates potential risks associated with each recommendation, helping investors manage their portfolio risk.

- **Data-Driven Insights:** Investors gain insights into market trends, patterns, and indicators that influence stock prices, enhancing their understanding of the market.

- **Continuous Monitoring:** Real-time updates ensure that recommendations remain relevant and responsive to changing market dynamics.

In conclusion, the Stock Market Recommendations Use Case demonstrates the application of data analysis and machine learning in providing personalized, data-driven investment advice to individuals looking to navigate the complexities of the stock market. This use case empowers investors with valuable insights and recommendations to optimize their investment strategies.

USE CASE #2 CODE: Stock Market Recommendations

```
#CODE STARTS

import streamlit as st

import openai

import yfinance as yf

import pandas as pd

import matplotlib.pyplot as plt

# Set page title

st.title('Real-time Stock Market Data Analysis with Azure OpenAI GPT')


# Create a text input for entering the stock symbol

stock_symbol = st.text_input('Enter a stock symbol (e.g., AAPL)')

# Set up Azure OpenAI GPT

# Set up Azure OpenAI GPT

# Authenticate with OpenAI API

openai.api_type = "azure"

openai.api_base = 'https://testgpt9212.openai.azure.com/'

openai.api_version = "2023-03-15-preview"

#openai.api_key = 'xxxxxxxxxxxxxxxxxxxxxxx'

openai.api_key = st.secrets['path']

#model_engine = "code-davinci-002"

gpt_model = "text-davinci-003" # Azure OpenAI GPT model
```

```python
# Create a function to generate a textual summary using Azure OpenAI
GPT

def generate_summary(symbol, data):

 # Implement your logic to generate the summary using Azure OpenAI
GPT

 # You can analyze the stock market data and generate a summary based
on the trends, news, or other factors


 # Example placeholder logic:

 summary = f"This is a summary for stock symbol {symbol}. The stock has
shown an upward trend in the recent days, driven by positive news about
a new product launch. Analysts are optimistic about the future
performance of the stock. However, it is important to note that stock
market trends are subject to change based on various factors."

 return summary


if stock_symbol:

# Load stock data

stock_data = yf.download(stock_symbol)


if not stock_data.empty:

# Display the stock data

st.subheader('Stock Data')

st.write(stock_data.tail())
```

```python
# Generate textual summary using Azure OpenAI GPT

if st.button('Generate Summary'):

# Perform text generation using Azure OpenAI GPT

summary_text = generate_summary(stock_symbol, stock_data)


# Display the generated summary

st.subheader('Generated Summary')

st.write(summary_text)


# Visualize the stock data

st.subheader('Stock Data Visualization')

plt.figure(figsize=(10, 6))

plt.title(f'{stock_symbol} Stock Price')

plt.plot(stock_data['Close'])

plt.xlabel('Date')

plt.ylabel('Price (USD)')

st.pyplot(plt)


# Perform analysis on the stock data

st.subheader('Stock Data Analysis')


# Calculate and display the simple moving average (SMA)
```

```python
sma_period = st.slider('Select SMA period', min_value=5, max_value=50,
value=20)

stock_data['SMA'] = stock_data['Close'].rolling(sma_period).mean()

st.write(stock_data.tail())



# Calculate and display the moving average convergence divergence
(MACD)

exp_short = st.slider('Select MACD exponential moving average (short)',
min_value=5, max_value=20, value=12)

exp_long = st.slider('Select MACD exponential moving average (long)',
min_value=21, max_value=50, value=26)

exp_signal = st.slider('Select MACD exponential moving average (signal)',
min_value=5, max_value=20, value=9)

stock_data['EMA_short'] = stock_data['Close'].ewm(span=exp_short,
adjust=False).mean()

stock_data['EMA_long'] = stock_data['Close'].ewm(span=exp_long,
adjust=False).mean()

stock_data['MACD'] = stock_data['EMA_short'] -
stock_data['EMA_long']

stock_data['Signal'] = stock_data['MACD'].ewm(span=exp_signal,
adjust=False).mean()

st.write(stock_data.tail())



else:

st.warning('Stock data not found. Please enter a valid stock symbol.')
#CODE END
```

Section 13.3: USE CASE #3 : Building Chatbots with OpenAI and Azure OpenAI[37]

Definition:

The Building Chatbots with OpenAI and Azure OpenAI Use Case involves the creation and deployment of conversational agents, also known as chatbots, using OpenAI's language models and leveraging the capabilities of Azure OpenAI services. This use case aims to provide businesses with intelligent and interactive chatbot solutions to enhance customer support, automate tasks, and improve user engagement.

Input :

- Enter : Questions

Output :

It generate answer

Software used :

- Python

- Streamlit

---

[37] All the use cases code download available : https://github.com/books-code/books-openai.git

- OpeanAI / Azure OpeanAI

Use Case #3 :

Scenario: A company in the e-commerce industry wants to improve its customer support services by implementing a chatbot that can handle customer inquiries, provide product recommendations, and assist in order tracking.

1. Chatbot Design: The company defines the scope and objectives of the chatbot, including the types of inquiries it should handle, the tone of communication, and the integration with existing systems.

2. OpenAI Integration: The company utilizes OpenAI's language models to develop the chatbot's conversational capabilities. The models are trained to understand natural language and generate contextually relevant responses.

3. Intent Recognition: The chatbot is trained to recognize different user intents, such as inquiries about products, order status, returns, and general questions.

4. Response Generation: The chatbot leverages OpenAI's language models to generate accurate and helpful responses to user queries. It can also provide product recommendations based on user preferences and historical data.

5. Integration with Azure OpenAI: Azure OpenAI services are used to deploy and manage the chatbot, ensuring scalability, security, and performance optimization.

6. Multi-Channel Deployment: The chatbot is deployed across various communication channels, such as the company's website, mobile app, and social media platforms, to provide seamless interactions with users.

7. Natural Language Processing: The chatbot employs natural language processing techniques to understand user inputs, including synonyms, variations, and colloquial language.

8. Contextual Conversations: The chatbot maintains context throughout the conversation, enabling it to provide relevant responses even in complex interactions.

9. Continuous Learning: The chatbot is designed to learn from user interactions over time, improving its accuracy and effectiveness in providing responses.

10. User Analytics: Azure OpenAI provides analytics and insights into user interactions, allowing the company to analyze user behavior, identify trends, and make informed improvements.

Benefits:

- **Improved Customer Support:** The chatbot offers 24/7 customer support, reducing response time and enhancing user satisfaction.

- **Task Automation:** The chatbot automates routine tasks such as order tracking, thereby freeing up human agents to focus on more complex queries.

- **Personalization:** The chatbot uses historical data to personalize interactions and offer tailored recommendations to users.

- **Consistent Responses:** The chatbot ensures consistency in responses across different channels, maintaining the company's brand image.

- **Scalability:** Azure OpenAI's deployment capabilities enable the chatbot to handle high volumes of interactions without compromising performance.

- **Data-Driven Insights:** Analytics provide valuable insights into user behavior, preferences, and pain points, aiding in business decision-making.

- **User Engagement:** Interactive conversations with the chatbot enhance user engagement and create a positive user experience.

- **Cost Efficiency:** The chatbot reduces the need for a large customer support team, resulting in cost savings.

In conclusion, the Building Chatbots with OpenAI and Azure OpenAI Use Case showcases the integration of advanced language models with cloud deployment capabilities to create intelligent and interactive chatbots. This use case empowers businesses to provide efficient customer support, automate tasks, and engage users in meaningful conversations across multiple channels.

USE CASE #3 CODE: Building Chatbots with OpenAI and Azure OpenAI

```python
# CODE START
import streamlit as st
import openai

# Set up OpenAI API credentials
openai.api_key = 'YOUR_OPENAI_API_KEY'

# Streamlit app title and description
st.title("Chatbot with GPT-3")
st.write("Type your message below and the chatbot will respond.")

# User input text box
user_input = st.text_input("You:", "")

# Generate response from GPT-3
if user_input:
 response = openai.Completion.create(
 engine="text-davinci-003",
 prompt=user_input,
 max_tokens=50 # Limit response length for a concise answer
 )
 bot_response = response.choices[0].text.strip()
 st.text("Bot:", bot_response)
#CODE END
```

Conclusion

In conclusion, this comprehensive guide has been meticulously crafted to empower you with a thorough grasp of OpenAI and Azure OpenAI services within a mere 36 hours. Whether you're a seasoned professional aiming to amplify your AI expertise or an enthusiastic newcomer eager to plunge into the realm of artificial intelligence, this book stands as your ultimate and indispensable companion.

Within the pages of this guide, you've encountered meticulously detailed instructions, pragmatic exemplars, and hands-on exercises – a dynamic combination intended to accelerate your learning trajectory. From forging a robust understanding of AI's fundamentals, OpenAI's intricacies, and the landscape of Azure OpenAI & Machine Learning, to embarking on the voyage of natural language processing and crafting interactive chatbots, you've embarked on a journey of knowledge that's primed for real-world application.

Author's strategic approach, meticulously outlined throughout these chapters, guarantees that each moment invested is maximized. Every section, building upon its predecessor, unearths layers of comprehension and cultivates pragmatic competencies. The culmination of this 36-hour odyssey will leave you fortified with a robust bedrock in OpenAI and Azure OpenAI, bestowing upon you the potency to wield these avant-garde technologies with efficacy and innovation.

As you conclude this journey, rest assured that the skills you've garnered are poised to make an impactful mark in your professional trajectory. OpenAI and Azure OpenAI are formidable tools, and now you're equipped to harness their potential in a multitude of applications. The culmination of these 36 hours is not an end, but rather a pivotal juncture – one where your newfound insights are poised to inspire and propel your AI endeavors.

Author's End Note

In closing, I extend my heartfelt appreciation to you for embarking on this enlightening journey through the world of OpenAI and Azure OpenAI services. As you reflect on the knowledge gained, remember that the realm of artificial intelligence is ceaselessly evolving. Embrace the curiosity that brought you here, and continue to explore, experiment, and innovate.

This guide is but a stepping stone, a foundation upon which you can build a world of possibilities. The OpenAI community and the broader AI landscape are teeming with potential, awaiting your creative touch. Whether you're delving into research, solving complex problems, or inventing new applications, remember that each insight you gain contributes to the ever-growing mosaic of human achievement.

As you proceed, we encourage you to remain curious, persistent, and bold. May your endeavors be marked by breakthroughs, collaborations, and a profound impact on the world. And should you find yourself seeking guidance or inspiration, remember that the journey of learning is a perpetual one, and the path forward is illuminated by your curiosity and passion.

Thank you for entrusting us with a portion of your learning journey. May your exploration of OpenAI and Azure OpenAI lead you to new horizons and uncharted territories. Here's to your continued success and the remarkable AI-driven future that you're shaping.

About the Author

Ajit Dash is a seasoned professional with over 24 years of experience in data and analytics. He has held various roles, including Senior Director of Data, Cloud Advisor, Solution Architect, and Data Scientist Lead. Ajit specializes in providing enterprise and cross-platform integration solutions to corporations across industries such as Telecommunication, Biotech, Finance, Banking, Media, Aerospace, Insurance, and Technology.

Ajit's expertise includes AI , Generative AI, Enterprise Solution Architecture, Cloud Advisory, Data Lake, Big Data, Data Science, Data Warehousing, Database Management, and BI Reporting. He has collaborated with clients like Microsoft, Fox, Oshkosh, Otis, Travelers, Apple, Qualcomm, IBM, and LPL Fin.

Ajit holds a master's degree in general management from Harvard University and a master's degree in computer information systems from the University of Phoenix. He also has a bachelor's degree in electrical engineering from India.

Ajit is passionate about sharing his knowledge and insights. He maintains a blog called "The Data World" (http://www.thedataworld.org), where he publishes articles, tutorials, and industry insights related to data, analytics, and emerging technologies.

With his extensive experience and technical skills, Ajit Dash continues to make significant contributions to the data and analytics field, empowering organizations to leverage the power of data for informed decision-making and strategic growth.